ARRIVING TO

the Lighter

SIDE OF LIFE

Journey and Destination

A. AMALFITANO

Trilogy Christian Publishers

A Wholly Owned Subsidiary of Trinity Broadcasting Network

2442 Michelle Drive

Tustin, CA 92780

For information, address Trilogy Christian Publishing

Rights Department, 2442 Michelle Drive, Tustin, Ca 92780.

Trilogy Christian Publishing/ TBN and colophon are trademarks of Trinity Broadcasting Network.

For information about special discounts for bulk purchases, please contact Trilogy Christian Publishing.

10 9 8 7 6 5 4 3 2 1

Library of Congress Cataloging-in-Publication Data is available.

ISBN 979-8-89041-649-0

ISBN 979-8-89041-650-6 (ebook)

2

To all those whose life has been

shattered along the way…

ACKNOWLEDGMENTS

I am eternally grateful to my daughter-in-love, Erica Amalfitano, for being my sounding board for years as I imagined and discussed the writing of this book, as well as her many edits, direction, and encouragement. She was my "Barnabas" throughout the process.

This next list of thanks is long because these are the people I have grieved for in my life and those who have grieved with me and been my support and anchors within my grief and trauma.

But first, my very existence and creation of this book is at the guidance of my Lord King Jesus, who always gave me beauty for ashes, joy in my sorrow, peace in my chaos, clarity in confusion, and comfort when I felt inconsolable!

To my beloved husband of thirty-one years, and friend of thirty-four years, Abe Amalfitano. Together, we walked through many of life's challenges that brought immense joy and sorrow at times. He demonstrated his love for me daily, had an unforgettable laugh, and a heart of gold. Your presence is missed daily!

To my mother, Mary Legato, who was the wind beneath my wings. She was and will always be the most amazing woman I know. Born in 1930 and left in the vestibule of the New York Foundling Home in Manhattan, she never knew her parents, her true birth date, her real name, or her ancestry. She spent many years in foster care, never truly accepted, and always made to feel like an outsider, yet she was loving, caring, and self-sacrificing till she passed at the age of eighty-three. She was known by my friends as "Moma Mary" and loved by all who came in contact with her. She was an amazing cook and singer, gracious in every way, beautiful, and filled the role of mother, father, and best friend in my life. Her essence made a difference in this world, and her companionship is deeply missed.

Beyond measure, overflowing thanks to my children, Jackie, Jesse, and Luke, who shared the loss of father, grandmother, uncle, and others that we loved. Together, we walked through many moments and hardships in life that brought sorrow, and yet *you all* gave me strength, encouragement, and support that goes beyond words. I would be amiss not to mention their spouses and my greatest joys... my grandchildren. They are uniquely and wonderfully made and are the rarest of gems. Their love and resilience are a constant driving force for me to be the best mother and grandmother I could be. Thanks to my brother, Gaetano Caserta, my nieces (their spouses), and my great nieces. Together, all of us affect and influence each other as we share experiences and memories. We lean on and glean from the strength of our family ties and show the world that family is God's design, and He did well when He chose all of you for me!

A special shout-out to my granddaughter Evey Bella Amalfitano, who helped me with the wording of the title of this book when I couldn't decide. I gave her the choices, and without hesitation, she chose its final name.

My final gratitude is to my friends of over fifty, forty, thirty, and twenty years. As with my family, you have walked by my side through the majority of all my experiences. Friendships have deep roots as the years turn into decades. So, to you, my friends (my family, too), I want to thank you for your ears, your shoulders, your time, your love, your support, your embrace, your tears, your laughs, your advice, and your patience with my talkative nature and many flaws and failures. You, as my family, are the audience that has been with me and has cheered me on through life's ins and outs and ups and downs. You have shared many of the darkest and lightest moments that have shaped me, thereby shaping this book, and I am forever grateful!

Lastly, I believe that friendships are like flowers and trees; some are stunningly beautiful but last only a few seasons and fade away, but others have a different beauty that renews each year and continues to grow deeper in the depths of the earth, like a redwood, and will withstand the fiercest of storms. God has graciously blessed my life with the latter, and you are treasured.

TABLE OF CONTENTS

PREFACE

This book was motivated by my personal loss, grieving of loved ones, childhood trauma, and the desire to help those like me, or even worse than me, trying to navigate through life despite and in spite of all the inevitable challenges in life in a fallen world. I trust God has given me the wisdom and words written here to encourage you. I believe my desire to help has been lifelong with different pictures of what that could look like; however, in the last decade, the vision has become a little more focused. I gathered writings, thoughts, notes, and scribbles that were in my journals and computer for years, began compiling and writing this book, and completed my BAS in Psychology/Christian Counseling from Liberty University.

I am not a licensed counselor; however, I have been a student of God's Word for over three decades, working toward certain certifications and my master's in clinical counseling. I also sit on the board of directors of The Starfish House in DeLand, Florida, a home for women, and provide biblical guidance. I have led several biblical group studies, including codependency behaviors and grieving, as well as individual biblical counseling since 2016.

As I was coming close to finishing my writing, or so I thought, a dear pastor friend and woman I am in ministry with asked me if I would counsel a group of ladies from her church who had recently lost their husbands and several who had been widowed for a bit. I extracted much of the material from my book, added thoughtful reflection questions with the help of my daughter-in-love, and turned it into a Bible study. During the fall of 2020 into the winter of 2021, I met with nine wonderful women who had endured much in recent years, as well as many years before. We cried, laughed, studied God's Word, encouraged and healed together.

Early on, I realized there are many dark places in life that trap us, and a person does not have to experience death to be in a holding pattern, ruminating about past trauma, or unable to function in life's daily activities because of it. Or worse, you are hiding your pain and sinking daily, as if standing on quicksand. You may have bought this book due to the loss of a loved one, and I pray every word reaches into the darkest part of your heart and mind and shines a flicker of light that draws you to it. However, this is also for the one who is currently experiencing or trying to move as far away from the below traumas as possible.

◊ Abandonment

◊ Child or adult homelessness

◊ Sexual abuse

◊ Physical abuse

◊ Orphanage

◊ Human trafficking

◊ Surviving a terrorist attack such as 9/11 or an environmental disaster

◊ Suffering from PTSD

◊ Multiple traumas

◊ Or one or more of the above simultaneously.

My perspective, personal experience, and position are viewed through the lens of Christianity: God the Father of Abraham, Isaac, and Jacob, as my heavenly Father, Jesus as my Lord and Savior, and the Holy Spirit as my comforter, counselor, and teacher who gives me peace and the ability to overcome unbearable pain, by the blood and resurrection of Jesus!

The Bible consists of sixty-six books that are without error and contain instruction, wisdom, teaching, and direction for any and all circumstances of life. There is nothing new under the sun… God covers it all; nothing is hidden from His sight, and there is nothing that you or I can do that He cannot or will not heal. He restores all that life has stolen from you and makes you whole again. We need only ask, and it will be given; He is an amazing God, Father, and Savior.

I have laid out some biblical truths that are foundationally for *Arriving to the Lighter Side of Life* no matter where you currently are, and although I have not experienced all the traumas I listed above, I have some of them and will share my experiences. My guidance has prayerful consideration, biblical backing, and pure, heartfelt love for your restoration and wholeness.

When I use the word "grief" or "mourn," it refers to whatever life trauma that has caused you to grieve or mourn your life, as well as, or in addition to, the loss of a person from death or divorce. Grieving and mourning are the feelings that result from the loss or trauma. We are talking about anything that has caused you to be stuck in… *post-traumatic life living* (ptll)!

Drug and alcohol addictions are self-inflicted by-products of the trauma that has occurred. The above list is out of a person's control: things that were done to them by others, environmental occurrences, and acts of terrorism. It is the trauma that causes us to turn to addictions or to intensify them during ptll, along with other vices: pornography, immorality, infidelity, etc. This book organically has these challenges in its underlying message and will be addressed in generalities; however, if these challenges are destroying your life, then seek advice from a licensed psychologist or substance abuse counselor who uses biblical counseling.

Losing a loved one or struggling to overcome a life trauma can feel like your heart is going to implode inside your body; it aches, it longs, and it breaks down in the deepest part that you never felt before or even knew existed. Your emotions are betraying you... at times, you cannot catch your breath, stop crying, get off the couch, talk to anyone, including other loved ones, have intimacy with your spouse, be a part of your children's day-to-day events, cook a meal, exercise, join in family activities, go to church, listen to certain music, and even walk the dog, etc. Completing daily tasks seems as if you are climbing Mount Everest! Is this normal behavior, how long should this last, and when is it no longer normal behavior?

There is a journey and destination—a journey from your current behavior because of the trauma to arriving at your new destination. The journey is where we work through the hurt and pain; it is a purpose-driven walk through the darkness of our souls, where hidden secrets and frightening visions are comfortable staying but causing your world to stay in the shadows. Once exposed, the light will always overtake the darkness. It is also described as hugging the cactus or letting the bear out. Regardless of the label, my prayer is that you will find hope in these pages that will provide peace on your journey of arriving to the lighter side of life.

Life grief and trauma are inevitable, intimately individual, and indiscriminate in length of time, no matter what your worldview is.

Regardless of your race, faith, lack of faith, gender, or age, my goal is to impart insight, compassion, and love to you. My profession of faith is so that you know my heart and that I will give you the best guidance, based on Scripture and experience, as you navigate through life grief and trauma or help another through their grieving and trauma. My guidance will be grounded in the inerrant Word of God, which teaches all mankind, male and female, that we are created by Him in His expressed image. Even if you do not believe in God, or you are unaware of His presence in your life through Jesus and the Holy Spirit, it does not mean *He is unaware of your life grief and trauma and not willing and waiting to provide comfort at your asking! His breath was your first breath of life, and He loves you beyond your wildest imagination!*

— Chapter 1 —

GRIEF IS INEVITABLE

"And inasmuch as it is appointed for men to die once and after this comes judgment" (Hebrews 9:27, NASB).

"No man has authority to restrain the wind with the wind, or authority over the day of death; and there is no discharge in the time of war, and evil will not deliver those who practice it" (Ecclesiastes 8:8, NASB).

"Consider it all joy, my brothers and sisters, when you encounter various trials, knowing that the testing of your faith produces endurance. And let endurance have its perfect result, so that you may be perfect and complete, lacking in nothing" (James 1:2–4, NASB).

Grief and trauma are inevitable because physical death and life traumas are inevitable. Some people experience grieving for a loved one early in life, while others may go an exceptionally long time before they do. My first devastating loss was in July 1974, when a special friend died in a car accident. Then, in 1989, the passing of my younger brother had me on a roller coaster that was spiraling downward, out of control for a while! I was thirty-four, married, with three children, and felt alone, abandoned, and angry.

The grief I felt was debilitating, destructive, and long-lasting (about five years). Beyond that, I had to watch my mother grieve her son, her baby! I believe that was my saving grace from totally losing it. I needed to be okay and strong for her. Even though I was a Christian, at the time, I had not fully surrendered my life over to Christ. I kept Him at a distance; I was still so sure that I could do it better, *and* I was incredibly angry at God. Over time, I understood that it was my brother's stupidity of doing drugs, not God's fault… God did not cause my brother's death. Yes, that happens to all of us, blaming God, and I am beyond thankful that I have been given the chance to ask for forgiveness for my anger, attitude, and behavior at that time of my life. It was not pretty!

🌿 *Grief does not fit into a box!* 🌿

There are levels of grief. The grief of a spouse is different than that of a parent, a child, a sibling, a best friend, and so on. Grieving the traumas in life is subjective; we will talk about this later on in more depth, but for now, being sexually abused by a parent, who is supposed to protect and nurture you, may be much more difficult to overcome than if it were a stranger.

We are part of a connected system with our family and friends through memories, both good and bad, with laughter, security, love, and a sense of attachment. When the attachment is broken, we experience anger, resentment, sadness, despair, resignation, and finally, detachment, which is the "new journey" without that person that we need to walk through.

We never get over the loss or trauma; we just readjust our thoughts of that person, situation, or event. When we lose someone, we have pictures of them, visit grave sites, make their clothes into blankets, talk to them as we go about the day, use "their" sayings, watch their favorite movies that you may have hated watching when they were alive, and remember the things they loved and hated. We make any connection that is personal and find peace and comfort in it. We rely on our faith, prayers, and memories, and those of us who believe in Christ for sure hope that we will see them in heaven someday.

> For we know that if the earthly tent which is our house is torn down, we have a building from God, a house not made with hands, eternal in the heavens. For indeed in this house we groan, longing to be clothed with our dwelling from heaven, inasmuch as we, having put it on, will not be found naked. For indeed while we are in this tent, we groan, being burdened, because we do not want to be unclothed but to be clothed, so that what is mortal will be swallowed up by life. Now He who prepared us for this very purpose is God, who gave to us the Spirit as a pledge.
>
> Therefore, being always of good courage, and knowing that while we are at home in the body we are absent from the Lord—for we walk by faith, not by sight—we are of good courage, I say, and prefer rather to be absent from the body and to be at home with the Lord.

2 CORINTHIANS 5:1–8 (NASB)

When we experience a tear in our connected family/friend system, we must process it over time. Outlined by Tim Clinton, Archibald Hart, and George Ohlschlager in *Caring For People God's Way*, there are five stages of grief: denial, anger, bargaining, depression, and acceptance. It is healthy to go through these stages.

> The process of grief is just that—a process. Visualize the grieving process, not as linear stages to grow through, but rather as layers of an onion unfolding, or as a spiral, or roller coaster. Few experience the process in the linear way presented here. Many will report living one or more stages at the same time, or rolling through parts of the process, again and again (Clinton, Hart, & Ohlschlager, 2005, 366).

The unhealthy thing would be to stop at one of these stages and camp out! Please continue moving forward; do not plant roots; nothing can grow from this place; accept bitterness. It will not dishonor or berate the memory of your loved one. In fact, if they could communicate with you, they would be yelling, "Be happy! I love you! I am fine, and I need you to be!"

The same is true of any trauma; we need to readjust our thoughts about it, become aware of the triggers, and avoid them at all costs. If you were a victim of someone's evil intentions, moving forward removes their power over you, and it starts the healing process. I will be discussing ten foundational truths that will help you reset your mind and look to Jesus for your strength.

The five stages of grieving: denial, anger, bargaining, depression, and acceptance are all normal to experience. How long should they last? It depends, but on average, from one to three years. When is it no longer normal behavior? When you get stuck in one of these stages for a long period of time and are neglecting or unable to complete *everyday activities of life*.

During the time of post-traumatic life living, we must not forget or lose sight of those that are still in our lives and *count* on us! If you are a parent, especially a single parent, you need to be on point when they are around. They cannot comprehend the extent of what you are feeling, and you can't expect them to. They are looking to you for guidance, provision, answers, direction, and, most importantly, unconditional love. Your grieving might have to be when the children are in bed at the end of the day. On your morning drive to work, during your lunch hour, or your drive home. It is not easy when you must pick up the pieces of your life as well as others. Seek help; do not do this by yourself. Reach out to other family members, neighbors, and church members; if you are not affiliated with a church, join one, join a support group. Many employers provide counseling as part of the benefits package; take advantage of this. Prioritize time of solitude for yourself and do something you enjoy. I spent time with dear friends, gardening, reading, writing, praying, and doing one or two things that always made me happy and at peace. The goal is to arrive at the lighter side of life, which is finding peace in the aftermath of the loss or trauma.

I have lost many relatives/friends since 1989, including my biological father, my stepfather, and some of the most precious dear friends a person can have; however, the loss of my husband of thirty-one years on March 30, 2008, and my mother on October 25, 2013, shattered my world and placed it upside down.

❧ Let's reflect and draw on our faith ❧

If loss and trauma are inevitable in our lifetime at some point, how do we come to an acceptance of this, and how do we learn to live with inevitability in the everyday? Our mission is to learn how to walk through it without causing more devastation to ourselves and to those around us who are also affected, love us, and are hurting because we are hurting. Until a person experiences loss and trauma, it is extremely hard to understand or explain; we can only sympathize, listen, care, and be present when needed. Once again, if the mourning of the loss or trauma that you are experiencing is hindering you from everyday activities for an extended period, please seek professional counsel from a medical doctor or a psychologist, preferably one whose diagnoses will align with the Word of God.

The following are some reflective questions for you:

◊ Where are you getting support?

◊ How are you supporting loved ones who have experienced loss and trauma with you?

◊ Is your way of coping causing more devastation to those trying to support you?

◊ In which new ways have you readjusted your everyday life? New rituals, things you are avoiding, people you are avoiding, people you are clinging to or making new connections with?

Sometimes, loss and trauma create anger and blame toward God and feelings of faith abandonment, or they can create stronger feelings of faith. In what ways are you turning to God and showing up to your faith as a way of coping and finding peace through your days?

Chapter 2

GRIEF IS
INTIMATELY INDIVIDUAL

❧ Grief is intimately individual
because our experiences are subjective. ❧

If you have ever gone hiking on a trail in a state or national park, the trailhead usually has a trail map in an enclosed case with other important information about the trail and park. The trail map will have the route laid out with a key to certain stops along the way that you should be aware of. It is a helpful guide when mountain hiking on an unfamiliar trail. On most, there will be a big *X* in color that says, "You are here!" The day your earth shattered and the day your new journey began is after one of the following events:

◊ Your spouse, your parent, your child, your sibling, your relative, your friend, or anyone else has passed.

◊ You remembered what happened to you as a child.

◊ You can no longer keep your trauma inside; it is bubbling into every area of your life.

◊ You get divorced; you are estranged from a child or a friend.

◊ The worst… your loved one committed suicide or was murdered

No matter the reason, you are standing on a big X of an unknown walk that you must travel!

Greif is intimately individual because our experiences are subjective. From your X, you are blind to every emotion, situation, or circumstance you will encounter going forward and how you will react. You are on an unknown trail that has been traveled by a googolplex of people but is uniquely intimate because each of us carries mourning differently due to our previous experiences and how we filter life.

An experienced hiker who has traveled on a particular trail will be able to maneuver very differently than one who hasn't, and yet when you are recovering from loss and trauma, an obstacle that once was very easy to overcome becomes a monumental task. Mourning becomes a part of you for an unlimited space of time and can be gentle and easy flowing one minute, and in the next, a white-water rapids ride. The only guarantee you have is that you will reach the other side stronger and wiser than when you started. You will no longer be in post-traumatic life living; you will be in…

Praise the Lord Living! (PTLL)

In September 2019, I went to the mountains with my son, and we went on several hikes. Some ended at beautiful waterfalls, with a trail that was one way in and the same way out. Others were climbs that were up, around, and sharply down the mountain, along narrow ledges with amazing vistas. I am not a hiking aficionado, and depending on the area of the country you live, you may or may not have experienced mountain hiking at all. Hopefully, my words will give you a visual to tie your mourning journey as you travel through it. I would like to use two types of hikes as an analogy for intimate, individual grief. I want to preface this by saying that your mourning isn't one way or another; as a matter of fact, over the last fifteen years, since my husband Abe passed, I have experienced both journeys at different times for periods of time. Both are normal and quite possibly necessary for healing.

They work in conjunction, not separately.

Grief Climb—sometimes, it might be a quick, gentle climb in one direction, a careful downhill trek, while other times, it is a long, hard, exhausting upward climb. Going up and around a mountain has many terrains… upward inclines, steep downhills, rocky, dense, or narrow paths. Every moment, you are aware of the changes, and even though the unknown lies ahead, you plow through.

For perspective—you are now a single parent, dealing with children, school, work, and extended family alone, with no stopping, no reprieve! Occasionally, you reach a vista, beautiful, serene, a place where you can breathe (a breathtaking view). You linger there momentarily, reflecting on the hard road you just traveled. This climb includes all the "firsts" since your loved one has passed. First anniversary, first holiday, first "anytime" without a loved one. These "firsts" will come again, and you will go through them, putting one step in front of the other, maybe pensive, maybe uncertain, maybe unsteady, like a rocky terrain. Remember, you have never traveled this path before, and you are numb and possibly in self-preservation mode, blocking most of it out. This climb will also have those once-in-a-lifetime moments you will face: the birth of a grandchild, the marriage of a child/grandchild, graduations—the things that can only happen once—and the person you thought you would share that with is gone. Don't allow these celebrations to pass without enjoying them. Give yourself the respite; take a night, a day, or a weekend, if possible, before them to prepare. Do not feel guilty if you look forward to them; the person involved still needs to know they are important to you, even though your emotions are scattered, torn, and worn. You intend on moving forward, but take a moment, readjust, and refresh before moving on. Do something you love during hard times, something you always wanted to but never did for some reason or another. You are not being selfish; you are being self-aware of the energy you need to be present in every area of your life without that spouse, parent, child, or someone who has left a void.

This example is also the day that you decide that the trauma, whatever it was, is no longer going to stop you from living. Many "firsts" will occur going forward, such as your family and friends seeing you smiling again, accepting the invitation, not being angry at the world, and no longer in victim mode but in survival mode! You are putting the past behind you and taking the climb into the unknown. You are confident, strong, and accepting of what you cannot change and making the changes you can! The past is no longer going to keep you in bondage and stuck in ptll. You are over it, even if you aren't sure how it looks. It is like this climb; you don't know what the next twist or turn will bring, but you will keep moving forward.

❧ Your faith goes before your feelings. ❧

All majestic vistas look different on a sunny day as opposed to a cloudy one, especially at higher elevations. The morning light will give hues of color differently than the afternoon or early evening. The view in summer, fall, winter, and spring will take on a life of its own. Trees will be colors of green, brown, amber, red, and orange covered with flowers. The trees can be leafless or just show signs of new buds after a long, cold winter.

31

🌿 *So it is with mourning; your view of it*
will always be evolving as the seasons pass. 🌿

Grief Hike—you will be taking this path back again; there
is no choice: one way in, same way out! Every year, birthdays,
anniversaries, Thanksgiving, and Christmas will come, and
every year, you will face it with a different frame of mind. This
journey you might take more slowly, or be more conscious of
certain emotions, not to linger there right now, because you
know, with certainty, it will come around again. It reminds me
of the famous line of Scarlet O'Hara from the movie *Gone with
the Wind*. She says repeatedly, "I won't worry about this today;
I will worry about it tomorrow!" (paraphrased).

As you hike, you take note of a certain tree limb that crosses
the path like a bench and think to yourself, *On the way back, I
will sit awhile, or maybe next year, I will linger in this special
place.* If you are a rock collector like me, you are searching for
the perfect size and shape and placing it conspicuously so you
won't miss it on the way back. There is no way you are going
to carry it the whole way; it is too much of a burden the whole
trip, but partway, you can manage it. You are no longer numb;
however, you are carrying burdens that you never experienced

before. Maybe next year, you can bask in that occasion on a deeper level, remembering and smiling.

You are passing through life as you never imagined.

Void of the person: their voice, their support, their love, their encouragement, their presence!

Void of being a victim: the loneliness, the negativity, the insecurity, the fears, the feeling of powerlessness!

Over the past fifteen years, I have never gone through certain times of the year the same, and yet, at other times, I am not willing to change a thing about that time. When circumstances force changes, for whatever reason, it is hard for me to adjust.

For example, my husband's birthday… every year, I celebrate it with his favorite dinner, no need to change it, happy for the consistency. Christmas is always the same: traditional reminiscence.

My wedding anniversary and the anniversary of his passing are never the same from year to year. My preference is to do something completely different in a different place. The only consistency during this time is, I will go to the beach leading up to or right after it.

This behavior was not planned; it evolved as my grieving did. I had just become aware of the consistency and inconsistency of the pattern when I started to write about it.

❧ *Let's reflect and draw on our faith* ❧

If loss and trauma are intimately individual, how are we carrying it? Will we allow it to destroy us or make us stronger?

◊ How are you carrying your emotions?

◊ Are you hiding your emotions from others who are also experiencing loss and trauma, feeling vulnerable, and not wanting to share?

◊ By keeping your emotions a secret and making others think you are fine, are you helping or hindering them? Are they so focused on you that they cannot focus on their own healing?

34

— Chapter 3 —

GRIEF IS INDISCRIMINATE IN LENGTH OF TIME

How long should a person grieve or relive a particular trauma? Who determines the length of that time for a person? As mentioned previously, we can only gauge it by our behavior… how long have you planted roots in *post-traumatic life living* (pɫll)? How long have you been in the five normal stages of behavior? A decade, two, three? Have drinking, drugs, or other vices taken over your life to avoid moving forward? Have you alienated others? Have you been unable to hold a job or to support or be present in your family?

Are we hindering God's divine will to arrive at the lighter side of life?

Ultimately, my hope and prayers are for you to arrive at the destination of *Praise the Lord Living,* not post-traumatic life living, but for now… we are starting a new journey, trying to figure a new way, gain hope, be content, and live in peace. Grief and trauma can keep you deep in the woods of despair, feeling lost and vulnerable, with no resources and totally unprepared emotionally for what has occurred and how you have gotten to this place. The years are rolling past, and you are still standing on the *X*. If this is you, then reading this book is in God's divine will for you. This section is a little longer because I want to share two stories of two men who experienced life grief and mourning unlike any others I have ever encountered; Job and Joseph were men who faced their grief and trauma and trusted God under the most traumatic of circumstances. God then turned everything to the good for both, their future, and the Hebrew nation for many generations after them. Thank you for joining me!

🌿 *But first…* 🌿

My mom came to live with me five months after my husband died; she was also a widow, seventy-eight years young. I had prayed for years that she would relocate from South Carolina to Florida, and God answered that prayer. I was able to spend the last five years of her life with her. She passed in October 2013, and a few months later, I was walking on the beach, and I bumped into a dear friend that I had not seen in a few years; we had met at a Kay Arthur's Precepts Bible study—if you never have attended one nor heard of one, find one, join one, you will benefit greatly from it. Anyway, we chatted on the beautiful Florida coastline while walking, catching up on life, and when we parted, she hugged me and said, *"You will be a mess until you are no longer a mess."* I welcomed these words, which comforted me for many years, and even shared them with others.

Grief is indiscriminate in length of time because brokenness is subjective. A person may be dealing with one trauma, such as the first loss they have ever experienced, or it could be multiple levels of trauma. For example, the first loss could have been a violent death, losing more than one person at the same time, the loss of a child, the loss of your loved one killed on 9/11, a combat-related death, or a victim of Hurricane Katrina, or more recently, in Fort Meyers, Florida, Hurricane Ian, or any other natural occurrence that brings destruction or death. A person needs to deal with the initial loss but also the added levels of shocking violence and helplessness. There is no time limit on this type of grieving and trauma. Additionally, each of us is affected by the environment we came from or are currently in—being a victim of ptll or perhaps being exposed to multiple traumas, as listed above, over the course of our life can easily be piled on top of each other, blended and mingled into a tangled mess, and you can hardly breathe under the weight of it.

Do not gauge your grief within a span of time, *but* do not stand still in it either! Mourning can be sinking sand that will drag you into a bottomless pit. The only one that will join you there and rejoice in you being there is satan, the adversary. In fact, he is doing everything he can to keep you in an unhappy, unproductive, post-traumatic life living. You must let light in!

Call a friend or a hotline, get out in public, get a dog, get a hobby, join a book club, go to church, join a Bible study, go to the woods, take a walk, go to the beach, anything that will bring you out of your current environment. If you are unable to get out because of weather or a limitation, join an online group that will hold you accountable for just showing up. There are biblical counselors who will have phone conversations, video chats, etc., and there are connections you can make. Or I would welcome your emails: annie@hisguidance.com.

❦ *Job—A Blameless God-Fearing Man* ❦

I would like to share an amazing, true, biblical account of a man named Job. Theologians, pastors, biblical teachers, and others have many opinions about this book that vary; however, there's one main thing that is agreed upon: it is inerrant, inspired by God, and it shows us many lessons. First and foremost, it shows absolute true faith and trust in an unseen God, no matter how horrific the circumstances. It gives a glimpse of one man's faithfulness amidst tragedy and God's faithfulness to us.

The book of Job has an unknown author and is thought to have taken place in the patriarchal or prepatriarchal days before Moses due to the fact that it doesn't mention the Law or the Exodus from Egypt, and Job was offering sacrifices for himself and his family as opposed to a Levitical priest. The Levitical order was established by Moses and his brother Aaron was the first Levitical high priest.

I encourage you to read the entire book of Job, but I will summarize portions for you. Job lived in the land of Uz, which in the modern day is commonly thought of as a broad area to the South and East of Israel, including Edom, Moab, and Ammon.[1]

---

1   Bible Reading Archeology, "Where Was The Land Of Uz?," last modified April 14, 2016, https://biblereadingarcheology.com/2016/04/14/where-was-the-land-of-uz.

By all accounts, Job was known to be a blameless, God-fearing man who always turned away from evil. He had seven sons and three daughters and was considered very wealthy by the standards of that time and considered a great man. One day, the angels were gathering in heaven to present themselves before God, and satan was among them.

> The LORD said to Satan, "From where do you come?" Satan answered the LORD and said, "From roaming about on the earth and walking around on it." The LORD said to Satan, "Have you considered My servant Job? For there is no one like him on the earth, a blameless and upright man, fearing God and turning away from evil." Then Satan answered the LORD, "Does Job fear God for nothing? Have You not made a fence around him and his house and all that he has, on every side? You have blessed the work of his hands, and his possessions have increased in the land. But reach out with Your hand now and touch all that he has; he will certainly curse You to Your face."
>
> JOB 1:7–11 (NASB)

Satan, being the accuser of all men, was testing God and doubting the faithfulness of Job toward God. God gave satan permission to cause havoc in Job's life, but he was not able to end his life. Satan left the presence of God, and he began his evil. A great wind caused a house to collapse on Job's sons and daughters, who were gathered there, and killed them. The Sabeans and Chaldeans raided all of Job's livestock, killing them, and a fire fell on the sheep and the servants; all were killed except the servant who reported these tragedies to Job. In a single day, Job lost his children, oxen, donkeys, camels, sheep, and servants. Multiple trauma and Job's response was the following:

> Then Job arose and tore his robe and shaved his head, and he fell to the ground and worshiped. He said, "Naked I came from my mother's womb, And naked I shall return there. The LORD gave and the LORD has taken away. Blessed be the name of the LORD." Through all this Job did not sin nor did he blame God.
>
> JOB 1:1–22 (NASB)

41

Satan was not satisfied with Jobs' response, and he appeared to the LORD again, and once again, the LORD said,

> Have you considered My servant Job? For there is no one like him on the earth, a blameless and upright man fearing God and turning away from evil. And he still holds fast his integrity, although you incited Me against him to ruin him without cause.

> JOB 2:3 (NASB)

Satan proceeded to tell God that even though his children and possessions are gone, that may not be enough for him to curse God, "However, put forth Your hand now, and touch his bone and his flesh; he will curse You to Your face" (Job 2:5, NASB). So God gave permission to satan once again to attack Job, only to spare his life. Satan left the presence of the LORD and made boils appear from the soles of Job's feet to the crown of his head. Then, Job's wife began to ridicule Job and his integrity. She told him he should curse God and die! Job responded to his wife that a person cannot accept good from God and not accept adversity; once again, no sin came from

42

Job as he sat among ashes and scraped himself with a potsherd.

During one of the hardest periods of my life, when I was coming to grips with being a child victim of sexual abuse, dealing with a wayward child, marital problems, and financial lack, the book of Job was a constant encouragement to many truths. I was revisiting my Christian faith and learning to lean on the Lord amidst all the trials, and I hit a crisis of belief, where I had to unequivocally turn from the past to recommit, for all eternity, and surrender wholeheartedly to Lord Jesus, my King, and Savior! Several biblical truths became solidified within me during that time.

◊ God will turn all things to the good for those who love Him.

◊ My thoughts are not His thoughts, nor my ways His ways.

◊ He loves me, and I need to trust, wait, obey, seek His face, and pray.

◊ He is the same yesterday, today, and tomorrow.

◊ Unlike the time of Job, I have a Savior who sits at the right hand of God, interceding for me day and night to the Father.

43

◊ Satan has no power over me, as I am covered by the blood of Christ; satan has already been defeated at the cross.

God is the same yesterday, today, and tomorrow, and we have a few accounts where a holy, majestic, almighty God speaks directly to His creation. Job is one of the few *elites* who had a direct discourse with God. God spoke out of a whirlwind and a storm to him. I wonder about these things… did He leave the heavenlies, or did He remain in His throne room? Were all the angels present and gathered around to hear this amazing example of love to one fragile human as God attested to His power, His presence, His marvelous workmanship, and the intricacy of creation? Did He summon satan to witness another battle lost, which were many already and many to come?

God questions Job as to his understanding of how the foundations of the earth were laid, its measurements, its heavens, its oceans, the light, the darkness, the boundaries, and who commands the boundaries. Who tells the waves to stop on the shore? Who commands the sun and the moon to stay in their place to rise and set? Where does light or darkness dwell? He asks Job if he ever walked in the deep recesses of the oceans or entered the storehouses of hail, frost, and snow.

I loved the ESV version of this portion of Scripture.

> Then the LORD answered Job out of the whirlwind and said:
>
> "Who is this that darkens counsel by words without knowledge? Dress for action like a man; I will question you, and you make it known to me.
>
> "Where were you when I laid the foundation of the earth? Tell me, if you have understanding. Who determined its measurements—surely you know! Or who stretched the line upon it? On what were its bases sunk, or who laid its cornerstone, when the morning stars sang together and all the sons of God shouted for joy?
>
> "Or who shut in the sea with doors when it burst out from the womb, when I made clouds its garment and thick darkness its swaddling band, and prescribed limits for it and set bars and doors, and said, 'Thus far shall you come, and no farther, and here shall your proud waves be stayed'?
>
> "Have you commanded the morning since your days began, and caused the dawn to know its place, that it might take hold of the skirts of the earth, and the wicked be shaken out of it? It is changed like clay under the seal, and its features stand out like a garment. From the wicked their

light is withheld, and their uplifted arm is broken.

"Have you entered into the springs of the sea, or walked in the recesses of the deep? Have the gates of death been revealed to you, or have you seen the gates of deep darkness? Have you comprehended the expanse of the earth? Declare, if you know all this.

"Where is the way to the dwelling of light, and where is the place of darkness, that you may take it to its territory and that you may discern the paths to its home? You know, for you were born then, and the number of your days is great!

"Have you entered the storehouses of the snow, or have you seen the storehouses of the hail, which I have reserved for the time of trouble, for the day of battle and war? What is the way to the place where the light is distributed, or where the east wind is scattered upon the earth?

"Who has cleft a channel for the torrents of rain and a way for the thunderbolt, to bring rain on a land where no man is, on the desert in which there is no man, to satisfy the waste and desolate land, and to make the ground sprout with grass?

"Has the rain a father, or who has begotten the drops of dew? From whose womb did the ice come forth, and who has given birth to the frost of heaven? The waters become hard like stone,

46

and the face of the deep is frozen.

"Can you bind the chains of the Pleiades or loose the cords of Orion? Can you lead forth the Mazzaroth in their season, or can you guide the Bear with its children? Do you know the ordinances of the heavens? Can you establish their rule on the earth?

"Can you lift up your voice to the clouds, that a flood of waters may cover you? Can you send forth lightnings, that they may go and say to you, 'Here we are'? Who has put wisdom in the inward parts or given understanding to the mind? Who can number the clouds by wisdom? Or who can tilt the waterskins of the heavens, when the dust runs into a mass and the clods stick fast together?

"Can you hunt the prey for the lion, or satisfy the appetite of the young lions, when they crouch in their dens or lie in wait in their thicket? Who provides for the raven its prey, when its young ones cry to God for help, and wander about for lack of food?[2]

JOB 38:1–41 (ESV)

---

2   "Job 38:1–41 ESV," Bible Gateway, accessed November 17, 2023, https://www. biblegateway.com/passage/?search=Job+38%3A1%E2%80%9341+&version=ESV.

Wow… as many times as I have read this portion of Scripture, it never loses its depth of meaning and wonder! It always overwhelms me with God's majesty.

While I was composing this section, I was at the beach and had just read a passage of Scripture in the book of Luke, which caused me to think further about God's conversation with Job, and I was moved to tears as I watched the raging Atlantic Ocean in front of me. I felt such a connection with Job's frailty and God's majesty. The passage I was reading described the day Jesus took His disciples out on a lake, and as they were sailing, Jesus fell asleep. While He was sleeping, a fierce gale of wind descended on the lake, and water started rising and entering the boat; frightened, they woke Jesus up, "Master, Master, we are perishing!" (Luke 8:24, NASB). Jesus rebuked the wind and the waves; they stopped, and everything was calm again. Jesus questioned their faith, and the disciples were amazed and said to each other, "Who then is this, that He commands even the winds and the water, and they obey Him?" (Luke 8:25, NASB).

I encourage you to take the time and read the full account of Job and be blown away and reminded of how blessed we truly are to wake up each day and to live each day to its fullest. We can view our world in the essence of love, beauty, wonder, and marvel as it was intended by our Creator if we only open our eyes, hearts, and minds.

Job 39–41 is God giving an account to Job about animals, mammals, birds, and all living things that He created and how they act, function, reproduce, and exist at His command. God also describes in detail the Behemoth and the Leviathan.

> Then Job answered the LORD and said, "I know that You can do all things, And that no purpose of Yours can be thwarted. 'Who is this that hides counsel without knowledge?' Therefore I have declared that which I did not understand, Things too wonderful for me, which I did not know." 'Hear, now, and I will speak; I will ask You, and You instruct me.' "I have heard of You by the hearing of the ear; But now my eye sees You; Therefore I retract, And I repent in dust and ashes."
>
> JOB 42:1–6 (NASB)

This scripture should be one that we live, breathe, and speak daily. God's creation is too wonderful for us to understand and fully know! I repent!

In the end, the LORD restores and increases Job's fortune. He was healed, and all his family came consoling, comforting, and giving him money and gold. His final days on earth were more blessed than his former, with many more sheep, camels, oxen, and donkeys. He had seven more sons and three daughters. His daughters were more beautiful than any other women in the land, and Job even gave them an inheritance along with their brothers.

"After this, Job lived 140 years, and saw his sons and his grandsons, four generations. And Job died, an old man and full of days" (Job 42:16–17, NASB).

Although Job struggled with accepting human suffering as part of life and was frustrated by it, as we all are, he would not take his wife's perspective to curse God and die. My hope is that you will find strength, hope, and truth in this story. That you will use it as a tool in your grieving process, knowing that God will restore you and your life. He is not done with you; just seek, ask, trust, and wait on His direction. Today, He speaks directly to us through the person of Jesus Christ and the Holy Spirit. Before Christ, there are many scriptures that describe, as above, God speaking using elements of nature: thunder, whirlwinds, storms, mighty winds, a burning bush, or His angels. Some theologians say that when the Scriptures refer to "the angel of the LORD," this refers to the preincarnate Jesus. I am in awe that He has so much love for us that He is always speaking, reminding us of His presence, power, and unconditional love.

Grief is indiscriminate in time, and we have no time reference on this portion of Job's life; how long did he wait before God spoke to him? How long did his three friends speak to and rebuke him, labeling him a sinner? (I did not share that portion of the story.) One can only imagine the grief and trauma Job might have felt for his first seven sons and three daughters. What I do know is that a day is as a thousand to the LORD, and a thousand is as a day.

"But do not let this one fact escape your notice, beloved, that with the Lord one day is like a thousand years, and a thousand years like one day" (2 Peter 3:8, NASB).

In the entire Bible, I do not know of any discourse between God and man that is more descriptive and beyond the imagination of man than creation! God's conversation with Job gives us a glimmer of His power and imagination in full force. His creation of the earth and all living things, in purity, beauty, and perfection as it was intended to be before the fall of Adam and Eve. This is how we are to view life and arrive to the lighter side of it and into praise the Lord living.

Time is irrelevant to the Lord. His view is eternal, and His purposes for your life were laid out before the foundation of the earth, so when you are in the middle of grieving, He is preparing you for His purposes in your future, not for that moment. Circumstances will give you the strength that you will need to catapult you to a new level for what you need later in life. Right now, it does not seem fair, or maybe you are going through the most horrific time you could ever imagine, but trust that God has a good plan for you on the lighter side of life.

God may allow tragedy in your life, but He will not allow it to stop the ultimate destiny He has planned for you.

God allowed satan to seemingly destroy Job and his family, but there is another story I would like to share.

Joseph, one of twelve sons of Jacob, son of Isaac, son

of Abraham, experienced life trauma and grief that was also indiscriminate in length of time. A father grieved for his son, and a son grieved for his entire family and former life for thirteen years before restoration occurred.

Jacob had two wives, Leah and Rachel, and his children were the leaders of the twelve tribes of Israel. Leah had ten sons with Jacob, and Rachel had Joseph and Benjamin. Jacob loved Rachel more than Leah, and after many years of Rachel being barren, she gave birth to Joseph. The name Joseph means "may He (the LORD) add."

Jacob's favoritism for Joseph was so blatantly obvious that his brothers hated him for it. Joseph was a dreamer and did not work in the fields, or anywhere for that matter. He was given *a coat of many colors* (Genesis 37:3). This coat and his constant dreams of lordship over the family made his brothers envy him to the point of hate. You might say he was beyond spoiled, entitled, and favored by his parents. One day, all the brothers were on a journey, and they devised a plan to kill Joseph; instead, under the advice and direction of the eldest brother, Reuben, they didn't kill him but lowered him into a pit and left him to die.

There is no record of how long Joseph was in the pit before a caravan of Ishmaelites found him and brought him to Egypt to be a slave in the house of Potiphar and eventually an official of the Pharaoh. At one point, Potiphar's wife made a false accusation against Joseph, and he was thrown in the royal prison. Remember his dreaming, what satan meant for evil, the accusation God turned to good. While in the prison, he interpreted the dreams of two officials, and eventually, he was brought to Pharaoh to interpret his worrisome dreams. Joseph predicted seven years of plenty followed by seven years of famine and recommended preparation for storing grain. Joseph gained so much favor from Pharaoh that he became second-in-command (Genesis 41:39–45). Who could have imagined this as a turn of events… from a death pit to second-in-command of Egypt! The famine brought people from all over to Egypt for grain, including Joseph's brothers. They did not recognize him, and as predicted in his dreams, they bowed before him. Joseph tested them several times before revealing his identity, and eventually, he was united with his father, and his entire family came to live in Egypt, in the land of Goshen.

Joseph, as second-in-command, could have destroyed his brothers for trying to destroy him. Years of separation from parents and home could have caused a root of bitterness to grow and take hold of Joseph's heart; he could have lived in the land of unforgiveness; instead, he wept, forgave them, and saved them from famine. Theologians believe that Joseph was seventeen when he was taken from the pit into slavery, and he was age thirty-nine when his family came to Egypt seeking grain. I suspect that from the moment Joseph was thrown into the pit, he was lost in a state of oblivion. He went from being the center of attention to a discarded person. Do you feel like that?

❦ Definition of "Oblivion" ❦

the state of being unaware or unconscious of what is happening:[3]

lost in oblivion

1. the state of being completely forgotten or unknown:

a former movie star now in *oblivion.*

2. the state of forgetting or of being oblivious:

the *oblivion* of sleep.

---

3   "Definition of Oblivion," Google, accessed November 17, 2023, https://www.google.com/search?q=defintion+of+oblivion.

3. the act or process of dying out; complete annihilation or extinction:

If we do not preserve their habitat, the entire species *will* pass *into oblivion.*[4]

Based on these definitions, I would say that Joseph went from being in oblivion to being lost in oblivion from his heritage and family. His entire lifestyle was lost; however, God had an ultimate plan: he and his brothers became the fathers of the twelve tribes of Israel, so no matter how lost Joseph was, God had him right where he needed to be to save not only his family, but Egypt, the nation of Israel, and the surrounding cities.

Do you feel lost in oblivion, a future you once were certain of is now unknown... you were a wife, a mother, a sister, a brother, a child, a friend, and now you are no longer any of these personas? This does not change the future from God's perspective, only yours. Joseph lay in the bottom of a pit, thought dead, unaware of his future, and yet he would be the one person who would save the nation of Israel from starvation.

---

4   "Oblivion," Dictionary.com, accessed November 17, 2023, https://www.dictionary.com/browse/oblivion.

You may be the one person who will save the future generations of your family.

He trusted, waited, prayed, and obeyed God. He did not stray from his faith, even when Potiphar's wife tried to seduce him, and he wound up in prison because he would not commit adultery, and she cried rape out of her rage. His life may have been spent in Egypt, but his traditions and faith would not allow him to disobey God's law and commandments. Joseph did not have Scripture to read, but he knew God.

Before the written Word, families spent evenings, work time, and any time telling their children the stories of God! Jacob and Rachel, his parents, would have told him their stories and experiences with God, along with what occurred in the lives of his great-great-grandparents, Abraham and Sara, and his grandparents, Isaac and Rebekah, and all generations back to the garden of Eden and his ancestors Adam and Eve. He came from the first man and woman of God's creation, a strong, long line of faithful people who told of the majesty and wonders of Yahweh.

I imagine if Joseph had access to the writings of the Psalms, he would have recited these verses in his state of oblivion.

57

Will Your wonders be made known in the darkness? And Your righteousness in the land of forgetfulness? But I, O LORD, have cried out to You for help, And in the morning my prayer comes before You. O LORD, why do You reject my soul? Why do You hide Your face from me? I was afflicted and about to die from my youth on; I suffer Your terrors; I am overcome. Your burning anger has passed over me; Your terrors have destroyed me. They have surrounded me like water all day long; They have encompassed me altogether. You have removed lover and friend far from me; My acquaintances are in darkness.

PSALM 88:12–18 (NASB)

Or perhaps Joseph would have recited this prayer/psalm of King David when he was confined to the cave.

I cry aloud with my voice to the LORD; I make supplication with my voice to the LORD. I pour out my complaint before Him; I declare my trouble before Him. When my spirit was overwhelmed within me, You knew my path. In the way where I walk They have hidden a trap for me. Look to the right and see; For there is no one who regards me; There is no escape for me; No one cares for my soul. I cried out to You, O LORD; I said, "You are my refuge, My portion in the land of the living. Give heed to my cry, For I am brought very low; Deliver me from my persecutors, For they are too strong for me. Bring my soul out of prison, So that I may give thanks to Your name; The righteous will surround me, For You will deal bountifully with me."

PSALM 142:1–7 (NASB)

How wonderful it is that we have all the writings of the faithful ones at our fingertips or at the sound of our voice… okay, Google! Those who lived before, during, and after our Savior, Jesus, witnessed direct signs and wonders individually or told by others who witnessed them. Yes, God did speak in a whirlwind, storm, a burning bush, by angels, messengers, prophets, Jesus Himself, the apostles, and even great historians like Josephus, but they did not have it all within their reach from beginning to end. They had glimpses but were unable to look back at the timelines and see the progression of faith. They forged the path with no real map, nothing played out, no reference point. They were on the path with no markers or guide,

59

no written instructions, except for the Ten Commandments and other Levitical laws. We have the completed map with all the symbols, scales, and keys…

◊   the mistakes

◊   the victories

◊   the captivity in Babylon in Egypt

◊   the cloud by day and the fire by night

◊   the silent years, waiting for the Messiah

◊   the persecutions

◊   the beginning of the church

◊   the pursuit of religious freedom at all costs

◊   the birth, death, and resurrection of our Lord

◊   the final destruction of satan and all evil

◊   our life after death with Jesus for eternity

They did not understand the message of the cross, the message of Christ, and His grace! They were waiting for the Messiah, and many still are. The Hebrew people did not accept Jesus when He came; even though they had all the prophecies predicting His birth, they were blind in their disbelief and in the world culture that they did not believe. So, it still is today; many are blinded by disbelief because they listen to the world and not to their heart. They do not open the Word of God and allow Him to speak, to trust the power of the Holy Spirit to counsel, convict, teach, and reveal the ways of our heavenly Father. Even though we have so many testimonies to strengthen and assure us in any and all circumstances, the noise, theories, precepts, and ideals of the world creep in and cause unbelief. The only way we can stop them is to have the Word of God, His Holy Word, speaking even louder. We must limit and control what goes into our minds to the things that are true and lovely and righteous and just and come from God and do not go against Him. It is not easy to shut the noise of the world out, go against the trends and what is politically correct, and stand for only what is biblically correct; however, it is essential for your peace and happiness to do exactly that. I may not know your specific situation, but I do know for certain that whatever it is, there is someone who has experienced it before you. You are never alone in your pain and suffering, and you need only seek God and trust He will guide you. He is the light of your path and will always lead you into the light and out of oblivion.

You are part of a bigger plan like Joseph was, a *God* plan ordained before the foundation of the earth, and only you can carry it out! It is designed for you; do not let satan steal it from you. Seek God's plan, wait, listen, watch, and pray. He will bring you out of the pit, out of your individual unique oblivion, into the light of His will.

❧ *Sitting with your life grief to move through it* ❧

Grief is indiscriminate in length of time because brokenness is subjective.

◊ Is your grief compounded by other unresolved traumas that have bubbled to the surface?

◊ Are you able to address these other traumas with someone to relieve some of the burden?

◊ By keeping your emotions a secret and making others think you are fine, are you helping or hindering them? Are they so focused on you that they cannot focus on their own healing from loss?

◊ In which new ways have you readjusted your everyday life? New rituals, things you are avoiding, new people you are talking to or connecting with?

◊   God may allow tragedy in your life, but He will not allow it to stop the ultimate destiny He has planned for you. In what ways are you turning to God and showing up to your faith as a way of coping and finding peace through your days?

— Chapter 4 —

FORGIVENESS FOR
SELF AND OTHERS

Before going further, I want to address the readers who are dealing with *lifelong trauma and grief.* You have been grieving your whole life: you were the innocent victim, never guilty of what occurred in your life… as a baby, child, teen, young adult, middle-aged, elderly… you were raped, abused, abandoned, tortured, treated inhumanely in some way, for a period, or just one horrific time. Or you were born to parents who never showed you love, and now you have no basis for loving others. You are standing on the big *X*, unable to move forward; as life moves, you are frozen in your life trauma and grief. You are in post-traumatic life living (ptll), and I want you to enter *Praise the Lord Living* (PTLL).

This is not easy, especially if you have filled your ptll with alcohol, drugs, pornography, and rage from the abuse that was done to you. When this happens, the response can be to treat others as you have been treated, so now you are the abuser of others. Having power over others makes you feel safe because you are in control of what you could not control in the past. There are many things we can discuss on this subject; however, I just wanted you to know that you are not overlooked in this audience. In fact, you may very well be the main audience. I want you to know there is hope for a different life other than where you currently exist. The darkest, deepest prison of despair and self-loathing, self-destruction, can be broken.

Let God's light penetrate the abyss, and He *will become the anchor in the tsunami of your life.*

I am going to give you a starting point, a tool, and permission to forgive yourself and those who wronged you. To move off the *X* by doing one thing before you open your eyes in the morning and as soon as you shut them in the evening. Just a few simple words will reach into the heavens, to the throne room of the Almighty Creator, the One who infused you with His breath, your first breath, your first heartbeat. Take a moment, feel that statement, hear it, believe it... don't run from it; let it linger.

The words are few and simple: *Lord, thank You for my life today; I surrender this day to You; go before me, forgive me as I forgive myself and others.*

In the evening: *Lord, thank You for Your protection today, forgive me, and may tomorrow bring joy that only You can give.*

This daily habit will transform post-traumatic life living to Praise the Lord Living!

Even if you wake up still high from the night before, hungover, reaching for the alcohol, the joint, or the snort to even function, do not open your eyes until you say the prayer! Before you pass out at night, say the prayer! Make this a habit for a day, a week, a month, a year, a decade, until you are reaching, desiring Jesus, and Him alone!

🌿 *Your faith goes before your feelings* 🌿

As discussed, grief is intimately individual, and so is forgiveness. This is a massive subject; it is subjective, heart-wrenching work. For now, we are only going to look at forgiving ourselves.

66

Self-unforgiveness can hinder the journey to the lighter side of life in an unhealthy, permanent way. Self-unforgiveness is one of the key elements that can keep you stuck on the X.

Reasons for self-unforgiveness:

◊ I am the one left behind.

◊ I should have seen the signs (a loved one committed suicide).

◊ I did not say things I should have.

◊ I said things I should not have.

◊ I caused the situation.

◊ I did not fix the situation.

◊ I did not get help in time.

◊ It should have been me.

◊ A parent should not outlive their children.

◊ I caused my children or siblings to stop speaking to me.

◊ I had an abortion.

Your circumstance…

When we forgive someone, we pardon them for a fault or offense. If we never get to tell that person we forgive them, or we are the offender, and we never received forgiveness, we carry the guilt. Self-unforgiveness means you are carrying the burden of guilt, and it permeates everything you do.

God is characterized as a God who both forgives and holds the guilty accountable. This is great news when we accept to surrender that control to Him when a loved one is no longer present to seek from or give forgiveness to turn to the only One who truly can!

> How blessed is he whose transgression is forgiven, Whose sin is covered! How blessed is the man to whom the LORD does not impute iniquity, And in whose spirit there is no deceit! When I kept silent about my sin, my body wasted away Through my groaning all day long. For day and night Your hand was heavy upon me; My vitality was drained away as with the fever heat of summer. Selah. I acknowledged my sin to You, And my iniquity I did not hide; I said, "I will confess my transgressions to the LORD"; And You forgave the guilt of my sin. Selah. Therefore, let everyone who is godly pray to You in a time when You may be found; Surely in a flood of great waters

they will not reach him. You are my hiding place; You preserve me from trouble; You surround me with songs of deliverance. Selah. I will instruct you and teach you in the way which you should go; I will counsel you with My eye upon you. Do not be as the horse or as the mule which have no understanding, Whose trappings include bit and bridle to hold them in check, Otherwise they will not come near to you. Many are the sorrows of the wicked, But he who trusts in the LORD, lovingkindness shall surround him. Be glad in the LORD and rejoice, you righteous ones; And shout for joy, all you who are upright in heart.

PSALM 32:1–11 (NASB)

The word "forgiveness" appears sixty-one times in the Old and New Testament.[5]

There are twenty-nine Bible verses on "forgiveness."[6]

The above are just numbers for a visual that we can gauge how important forgiveness is to God and the journey to be Christ-minded.

---

5   "Word Counts: How Many Times Does a Word Appear in the Bible?," Christian Bible Reference Site, accessed November 17, 2023, https://www.christianbiblereference.org/faq_WordCount.htm.
6   "Bible Verses about Forgiveness," DailyVerses.net, accessed November 17, 2023, https://dailyverses.net/forgiveness.

The reality is that the concept is much more powerful, and it can be the difference between arriving to the lighter side of life or being stuck in post-traumatic living, unable to forgive or accept forgiveness. God wants you to live life abundantly, and satan wants you to be in chains. The foundation of Christianity is forgiveness of humanity through the birth, death, and resurrection of Jesus Christ, the only begotten Son of God, born of the Virgin Mary, by the power of the Holy Spirit. A miraculous occurrence, designed by Jehovah God, before the foundation of the world to save us from eternal death and give us eternal life through the blood sacrifice of Jesus.

Our holy, heavenly Father—having foreknowledge but giving complete free will to His children—knew satan would never stop his evil intentions to destroy humanity, and He set a plan in place for a divine intervention that would seal satan's fate for eternity in the lake of fire. From the moment satan and one-third of the angels were cast out of heaven to the temptation of Adam through Eve in the garden up to today, his one desire is to destroy what God loves: humanity!

Remember, he prowls the earth looking for whom he can destroy and make fearful; he is a liar, and darkness follows him and all who follow him. Sly and cunning is his "modus operandi" to destroy marriages, families, and everything that God created; he does it by dangling power, greed, lust, fear, and distractions disguised as goodness, which only leads to destruction. Beware of the lion in sheep's clothing.

"Be sober-minded; be watchful. Your adversary the devil prowls around like a roaring lion, seeking someone to devour" (1 Peter 5:8, ESV).

The good news is, Christ took away the sting of death over two thousand years ago on the cross, giving the gift of forgiveness to *all* mankind; all we have to do is receive it and live for eternity in the light, able to withstand the schemes of satan daily. We are protected by the blood of Christ, armed with the power to defeat all temptations. Will we sin? *Yes*! We will always fall short, but once we accept Jesus Christ as Lord and Savior, His blood covers our iniquities, as far as the east is from the west. We are the righteousness of God through Christ, Hallelujah, Amen!

You may very well be feeling self-unforgiveness and guilt, and I say with much love and kindness that God, through Christ, planned for complete forgiveness of ourselves and others. To live in peace, guilt-free from all circumstances, by trusting His ultimate plan for goodness in our lives. I know this isn't easy when the voices in our head, opinions of others, and world culture scream the opposite to us, but start today right where you are, knowing you are accepted, loved, and forgiven. Our feelings deceive us, so change will not be immediate. It is a journey, an unknown hiking path to arrive to the lighter side of life. Each day, you will get a little closer to freedom, the burden you are carrying will be lighter, and slowly, you will move from ptll to PTLL. We all have a walk, a destination, a God-designed purpose; how we take that journey is totally up to us… so why not walk in happiness and peace? Christ gives freedom; satan gives bondage. Christ's blessed gift is for all men to have peace and joy in all the good things of the earth.

Your faith goes before your feelings

We have been talking about self-unforgiveness, but the same truths hold true when we have unforgiveness for another person. When we harbor bitterness, and our viewpoint of the person is tainted with hurt or even hatred. Maybe they are no longer here to ask your forgiveness or for you to forgive them, or maybe they are, but the hurt is too deep to even approach them.

God always has such perfect timing... Yesterday (June 2, 2020), while driving, Dr. Charles Stanley came on Cornerstone Radio Station, and his subject was forgiveness, and it made sense to me that a person can do the same with self-unforgiveness. (Dr. Stanley went to his heavenly home in May 2023, but his words of wisdom will live on for millions of Christians for many years to come.)

🌿 *The Two Chairs* 🌿

Get two chairs and sit them facing each other; sit in one and imagine the situation you will not forgive yourself for or the person you cannot forgive sitting in the other chair and begin to speak.

Express your anger, bitterness, deep hurt, regret, remorse, or any other emotion you have been harboring. As you release that person from your mind, your inner hurts will become free. A transformation will take place as you start to view that person or yourself differently; you will feel lighter, the bondage of an unforgiving spirit will fall away, and you will experience true freedom and love. There may be a reconciliation with a divorced spouse or family member that results from this experience, *but* maybe not. Maybe the person is no longer living, and you had no closure in their passing. Whatever the future holds is up to God, but you are now free from the bondage of bitter unforgiveness.

Example 1—you had an abortion, so you are speaking to your unborn child in the empty chair…

"Sweet child, I am so sorry I made the choice to end your life; a day does not go by that I do not think about who you would be today and how much joy, love, and amazement I missed out on that you would have brought to me and the world. There is no excuse that is valid now for what I did. Yes, at the time, I thought I had valid reasons, but I know now that I made a horrific mistake; I ended your life when I had no right to make that determination. God had a plan for you, and I interfered. His judgment is on me and me alone for my sin. You are well in His care, and I only hope that someday, He will allow me to see you and hold you in my arms. Please understand and forgive me so that I can forgive myself, and allow me to move forward, never forgetting you but letting others know the grief

74

that occurs when abortion is decided before it is too late for them. I will be an advocate for life! I know now that only God has the right from conception to allow life or death to occur. You were conceived in His image, and your name is written in the book of life, but because of my decision, you did not get to live! I am truly sorry."

Example 2—your spouse passed away after being sick for a long time, with you as the caretaker, and you are feeling relief mixed with grief. Or the sickness and passing was so quick, like in my situation, my husband was diagnosed and passed in twenty-seven days.

"The many months of taking care of you were difficult for me in several ways. I never could imagine anyone else doing this, but I needed a break so many times that I know you probably felt my anger. I am sorry that I wasn't more gracious, even if you didn't realize it due to your pain and sickness. I know the resentment I carried some days, not all days, but now that you're gone, just a few hours of that precious time, where I didn't cherish it, brings heartache. There have been times since your passing that I grieve for the hardest days and hope that I did not make you feel more pain, hurt, and discomfort than you already had. I may have been on autopilot instead of cherishing each second and not rushing through the tasks of care. Someday, we will see each other again, but I need to ask for your forgiveness now to say out loud what I could not express then. I love you... please forgive me."

This next example will be more personalized because it was my experience, but I know that many readers have had spouses who passed quickly. I did not struggle with self-unforgiveness as much as self-pity. Now, God did set me straight on that immediately; however, fifteen years later, I still have moments when seeing other couples aging together and having the life that I wanted to have with my husband. Having grown children with children, our grandchildren, retired, and having our freedom to grow old together.

"Your passing was like a blur; your sickness accelerated so quickly from hearing the doctor's words that you had stage 4 cancer in your lungs and that it had spread to your bones and throat to sitting in your memorial service twenty days later, I cannot remember one thing clearly that occurred. Yes, family and friends visited with comfort and love, but everything else is blank. The one thing that I do regret and hope that you did not feel hurt by was my not speaking in finalities in all our conversations over those few weeks. I could not give up hope for your healing, and I know you were sincerely seeking it. I remember wanting to say many things, but I felt you were dealing with so much I just wanted to keep things as positive and peaceful for you as possible. Within two weeks of your diagnosis, you were already so weak. I do remember in the weeks after your death thinking of things I wish I had said, and although the time did not ever seem right, forgive me if you needed it. I know you are having the best retirement a person could have. God assured me of that vividly, with His words from Psalm 84:10 (ESV): "For a day in your courts is better than a thousand elsewhere." I knew at that moment I would never question His will concerning you ever again. Thank you for thirty-three years (dating and marriage) of memories and family legacy to keep alive.

Example 3—a life of grief, trauma, or remorse—from birth, you have hated your life. You were unloved, neglected, abused, hungry, cold, abandoned, shunned, bullied, out of place in school, and always in trouble; everyone you see around you has a family, a home, but you come home from school every day to an empty, cold apartment, with no encouragement, no one to speak to, no one to share your day with. You have been starved your whole life of the necessities. Now you are an adult, passed all that, but the hurts and jealousies run deep, and you can see them coming out in all the areas of your life. You have a job but still feel like you do not measure up. Relationships are hard, and you are unable to maintain them for any length of time.

Pretend I am sitting across from you right now, and I want you to tell me everything; do not hold back. This may take several sessions; you have much to say, to scream and yell about. When you are finished being angry from all of your hurts and have said to me all the things you wish you could have said and screamed at your parents, teachers, school administrators, siblings, employers, friends, enemies, and strangers, then read and receive what I will tell you from my heart.

I want you to know that your childhood experiences are in the past, and they do not define you today but are the underlying strength that you can tap into whenever you need. You are a survivor and have endured with resilience all that has occurred. From this moment on, I am asking you to leave the past behind and do not look back. I do not want you to travel the loop path daily anymore; do not ponder the events, scenes, or feelings of that path any longer unless it is to remind yourself that you are no longer in that place. Do not filter today through the lenses of yesterday unless it is in a positive trajectory. God has a purpose for you, for your good, and maybe He will use your past to help another or to help you in your future. But right now, I am asking you to view yourself as a survivor… strong, capable, and not a victim of your past. You are no longer under the feet of satan; you are in Christ and viewed with love, grace, and mercy. He is your anchor, savior, and protector. I do not have the reasons for your beginning, but I know that your future is secure. I am asking you to trust and have faith that you are a child of God. God loves you; you are the head and not the tail, fully redeemed to walk in freedom and allowed to live beyond and above your circumstances with joy from this moment on. When the dark feelings creep in, which they will, squash them immediately. I am interceding on your behalf that no weapon formed against you shall prosper, and every tongue that revolts against you will be cast down in the mighty name of Jesus. Find one person that you can trust to stand with you daily and pray with you; if you have no one, reach out to me, and I will be the one: annie@hisguidance.com.

While writing this, I envisioned this example being spoken to a broken male, once a hurt young boy, which I find interesting, as the rest of the book seemed more female-specific. Maybe because I have two sons, maybe because I have witnessed the pressures and struggles of young men trying to be godly and ridiculed by society and labeled weak and wimpy. Regardless of my momentary feelings about your gender, your insecurities have hindered your ability to be monogamous and loyal.

God says to you the following: "The past ends now! Be faithful to Me, and let Me guide your next relationship. Pay attention to Me, lean on My Word, learn from My Word, and ground your every decision in My Word. I will turn your life around to the most amazing life you ever had the ability to conceive. The world's opinion doesn't matter, only Mine, and I made you in my image. With Me, all things are possible."

When you eliminate regrets, you eliminate undue pain and honor the sacrifice Jesus paid!

– Chapter 5 –

TRUTH IS AN ANCHOR, DECEPTION IS A TSUNAMI

Knowledge and Truth Are Vital Tools for the Journey

To arrive at the lighter side of life, you need to have the knowledge and tools to look beyond the trauma and learn God's plan for your life, maybe not this moment but the future. The way to start this journey is *to distinguish the truths from deceptions that may be currently guiding you in your life and to know and understand who your enemy is and that he has no power over you.*

Once you know and understand the difference, you can grow in these truths, as commanded by God, confirmed and solidified by Jesus, and inspired by the Holy Spirit. No matter where you are, as we have discussed… in the pit, on the climb, on the hike, or still standing on the X of your life trauma and grief... truth is truth, and you need to distinguish it from the lies and deceptions that satan has been permeating in our world for thousands of years. It is his strategy for waging war against God's children. He may win little skirmishes, but the battle has already been won, and the victory belongs to the Lord!

Truth and hope are the anchors of our lives; Jesus is the essence of both and so much more! Hebrews 6:19–20 (NASB) states,

> This hope we have as an anchor of the soul, a hope both sure and steadfast and one which enters within the veil, where Jesus has entered as a forerunner for us, having become a high priest forever according to the order of Melchizedek.

Hold tight to the anchor of your soul, Jesus; He is strong and steadfast. "Let us hold fast the confession of our hope without wavering, for He who promised is faithful" (Hebrews 10:23, NASB).

I ask you to take a pause in your trauma and look to your future, your eternal future after this life. We are grieving over those that left us, but they are not grieving over us, and we need truth to set us on the path of healing and wholeness. One of the important reasons, and probably the most important of all, is to be prepared for Jesus' second coming; it is inevitable, and knowing the signs, the truth versus the lies, will help prepare you and your loved ones. Jesus gave clear instructions concerning His second coming. He will return in the blink of an eye, and we need to be always watching for Him. It does not matter when it is; it only matters that we are prepared spiritually.

The truths that I will share are foundational for us to reach the lighter side of life and to grow in our relationship with Jesus and our Father God. God created us for a relationship, sacrificed His Son, and has justly, patiently waited for the fullness of time to come to bring a new heaven and new earth to completion where we will spend eternity worshiping and living with Him.

Unless you know the truth, you cannot recognize the deception or the counterfeit. Satan is the father of lies and is extremely crafty. He will purposely disguise the lie within the truth to deceive you.

Here are some definitions to help our understanding:

꧁ *Definition of "Truth"* ꧂

1.a.1. the body of real things, events, and facts: ACTUALITY

1.a.2: the state of being the case: FACT

1.a.3 (often capitalized): a transcendent fundamental or spiritual reality

1.b: a judgment, proposition, or idea that is true or accepted as true

> truths of thermodynamics

1.c: the body of true statements and propositions[7]

꧁ *Definition of "Anchor"* ꧂

1: a device usually of metal attached to a ship or boat by a cable and cast overboard to hold it in a particular place by means of a fluke that digs into the bottom

2: a reliable or principal support: MAINSTAY

> a quarterback who has been the anchor of the team's offense

---

7   "Truth," Merriam-Webster, accessed November 17, 2023, https://www.merriam-webster.com/dictionary/truth.

3: something that serves to hold an object firmly

> a bolt-and-nut cable anchor

4: an object shaped like a ship's anchor…

6: the member of a team (such as a relay team) that competes last[8]

🌿 *Definition of "Deception"* 🌿

1.a: the act of causing someone to accept as true or valid what is false or invalid: the act of deceiving

> resorting to falsehood and deception

> used deception to leak the classified information

1.b: the fact or condition of being deceived

> the deception of his audience

2: something that deceives: TRICK

> fooled by a scam artist's clever deception[9]

8   "Anchor," Merriam-Webster, accessed November 17, 2023, https://www.merriam-webster.com/dictionary/anchor.
9   "Deception," Merriam-Webster, accessed November 17, 2023, https://www.merriam-webster.com/dictionary/deception.

❧ *Definition of "Tsunami"* ❧

1: a great sea wave produced especially by submarine earth movement or volcanic eruption: TIDAL WAVE[10]

2: a very high, large wave in the ocean that is usually caused by an earthquake under the sea and that can cause great destruction when it reaches land[11]

Truth is real; it is a fact; it is actuality; it can be trusted, as an anchor, Jesus, holds it in place firmly. It cannot be moved, it is reliable, and it supports. Based on these definitions, truth is the foundation that upholds all questions; life is anchored in truth; it cannot be hidden or changed. It is true that the sun will rise and set every day. It is true that the waves will only go so far on the shore and then draw back. It is true that too much moisture in the air will bring rain and snow. It is true that we will all grieve someone someday, and we will all be grieved for by someone someday.

---

10   "Tsunami," Merriam-Webster, accessed November 17, 2023, https://www.merriam-webster.com/dictionary/tsunami.
11   "Tsunami," Britannica Dictionary, accessed November 17, 2023, https://www.britannica.com/dictionary/tsunami.

Deception causes someone to accept what is false as true or valid, deceiving a person or persons to believe a falsehood. Most times, the deception is disguised as a little untruth or a subtle change in things.

For a visual... the Earth has fault lines that lay under the seas, and tsunamis can be the effect of a volcanic eruption or an underwater earthquake by shifting tectonic plates. A natural shifting in the Earth's tectonic plates that is invisible to the naked eye caused the eruption. As the ground underwater shifts, cracks form on the seafloor, and from this movement, large waves form and reach as high as one hundred feet. *It is the underwater movement that goes unnoticed, and then it is too late to stop its full force of destruction.*

That is how deception works; it can start with the tiniest lie, such as "I deserve to have the attention of a woman, and my wife is too busy and tired raising our three children and caring for our home to give me that attention. The woman at work listens to me and is interested in what I have to say... I don't get this at home; I deserve to have some attention, etc. This affair means nothing to me, really, and I am not going to leave my wife; I just need attention." Then the affair starts, and before you know it, a family is torn apart, a marriage is destroyed beyond repair, it is shattered, and the children no longer have both parents under the same roof.

A tsunami has taken place because of a lie that the husband told himself. It probably took months to form the crack in the foundation of his marriage, but it erupted into a full-blown tidal wave that could not be stopped until it was too late.

There are many other deceptions in life that start off small or seemingly correct by the world's standards but destroy in exceptionally large ways because they are not God's standards.

As I was out walking, I noticed many cracks in the roadway due to the expansion and retraction of heat, traffic, etc. The cracks were all shapes and lengths, going in all directions. It got me thinking about how, after destruction occurs, scientists, couples, families, siblings, and people involved will try to piece together what happened to see clearly how it all started, whatever "it" is. In the infidelity example, if the couple reunited and entered counseling after the indiscretion, the counselor would possibly prompt them to see the prior wrong thinking and how the deception started... not to dwell there but for awareness.

88

After a tsunami, scientists will send divers to the ocean floor to trace where the eruption began and view all the cracks and splits it has made in the ocean floor. If our viewpoint is always in line with God and we weigh our actions in life from a biblical perspective, we will understand that there is always a spiritual side; we will see beyond the natural and find the buried truth.

In deception, there is always buried truth.

Finding the start of deception in the aftermath of destruction is reactive and much easier than being proactive. The signs can be easily traced back, and the pattern can be seen. Being proactive to avoid destruction takes a deep relationship with God, seeking His will to always avoid bad relationships or decisions from the start. It takes devotion to learning wisdom, faith, trust, patience, and waiting on God's will to be clear. Can destruction come even if you do all that? Most certainly, and all we can do at that point is to know that we did all we could and to trust He will turn all things for the good, for He promises this for those who love Him and are called according to His purpose.

🌿 *Life should be proactive, not reactive* 🌿

Being proactive in your life trauma and grief journey means paying close attention to things that trigger your sadness: conversations, times of year, places, smells, sounds, or being around certain people. I am not talking about having bittersweet memories that make you melancholy for a day or maybe two. I am talking about the storm cloud that is looming over you that limits your ability to function at home or work and causes you to be paralyzed in your daily activities or spend several days in bed, neglecting family and friends. Once you identify the triggers, you can detach yourself from them and decide to view them differently.

Awareness is the ability to identity the triggers that bring anxiety, stress, and self-doubt.

Away-ness is the ability to detach from the feelings or the people that bring on the feelings.

Affirming is deciding to rethink the way you previously thought and renew your mind.

I am not saying that you should not go through the emotional roller coaster that comes with life trauma and grief. Remember, you are on a journey that is inevitably in this fallen world, and it is healthy to go through the ups and downs, to take the climb or the hike several times. To work through emotions will allow you to become stronger with each go-around. What is not healthy is to dwell under the storm, under the covers, when the lightning and thunder are clashing, and you are immobile. Be proactive with the milestones that are upcoming and the triggers… change your environment, surround yourself with different people, and place yourself somewhere that will not allow the darkness to loom. This will help you be a healthier *you* in your journey to the lighter side.

You have precious memories; keep them precious, in the light, in a place of happiness to help you grow. Identify and become *aware* of the situation or issue that brings intense anger, sadness, guilt, or grieving; detach yourself, take yourself *away* from the thoughts, people, or the place that beings those emotions, and decide and *affirm* to yourself that you will no longer have the destructive, sad thoughts.

🌿 Jesus is the anchor and light of your life 🌿

I have a large collection of lighthouses, not only the ones that I collected but also my mother's. During the years she lived in South Carolina and I in Florida, we had both started collecting lighthouses, at first unknown to each other. I have always enjoyed displaying them on a mantle or glass shelves. They remind me to keep my mind on the light in all dark times.

Lighthouses line the coastal states of our country to guide ships into the rocky shores. Depending on the reefs and the break of the shores, the light from the lighthouses allows the captains to guide the boats safely around the rocks to the shoreline. Without the shining light from the lighthouse, it would be treacherous; the same holds true for our lives. Without Jesus, every move we make is a threat to our well-being. The lighthouse keeper's responsibility is to run the lights in the dark for the passing boats to maneuver safely to pass or to dock. Some shorelines are so dangerous that in turbulent waters, an anchor needs to be dropped in a safe place. A large ship will be unable to get through the rough waters, so a smaller craft will carry the ship's anchor through the breakers into the harbor to secure the ship. Jesus, as our light and our anchor, will give us direction, safety, security, and a firm hold during life's most difficult storms.

I am certain that once you understand the truths I am going to share and remain prayerful and intentional in your day, you will build a strong foundation to take small steps every day. This foundation will be strong and unwavering, and it will be your anchor and provide light in the darkness of times.

GOD, JESUS, AND YOUR RIGHTEOUSNESS

#1 TRUTH—A PERSON CANNOT SAY THEY KNOW GOD AND DISREGARD JESUS

No man comes to the Father except through the Son. "Jesus said to him, 'I am the way, and the truth, and the life; no one comes to the Father but through Me'" (John 14:6, NASB). Without this truth, a person has no foundation or ability to call God the Father! This is the Word of God, and it is all about Jesus!

Jesus is with God in the beginning.

Jesus is prophesied throughout the Old Testament.

Jesus is the fulfillment of the Law and Prophets.

Jesus was crucified.

Jesus rose from the dead.

Jesus is Savior and King then, now, and eternally.

"Jesus said to them, 'If God were your Father, you would love Me, for I proceeded forth and have come from God, for I have not even come on My own initiative, but He sent Me'" (John 8:42, NASB).

My writings are always based on the perspective and worldview that lies in the person of Jesus Christ and His authority above all things. There are many scriptures, spoken directly from Jesus, that attest to His position, supremacy, and authority to confirm that perspective.

My hope and prayer for everyone who reads this book is that they feel the genuine love and prayers that are behind every word, scripture, and thought. I will not address any truth or deception that is not written and confirmed in the Word or spoken directly to me by the Holy Spirit. Our world is facing unprecedented changes in culture that are affecting the morals, values, opinions, and divisions in the body of Christ, and we need to understand how to navigate through these challenges with love and unity; however, above all, we need to stand firm in our convictions and commands of God through the character of Christ.

There are many cultural challenges that the body of Christ is not in unity on; therefore, our response to these challenges has caused divisions among us. It is my desire to remind us of the truth of Christ versus the deception of satan to bring us into unity. Once the body of Christ can be as *one*, under Him, we can help the hopeless, helpless, hurting, addicted, starving, immoral, and deceived secular world. Jesus is in heaven, holding His arms out to us, wanting us to bring our weariness, hurts, disappointments, and burdens so that we can have rest for our souls. He is the anchor that holds the truth and leads us in life.

#2 TRUTH—YOU ARE THE
RIGHTEOUS OF GOD IN CHRIST JESUS

No man is righteous on his own account. We are all born into sin; however, the sacrifice of Christ paid our sin debt in full. Jesus took away the sins of all mankind when He died that day on Calvary. He died for all men, not some, not only a certain period, *all men, for all time*! What is unknown to all, except

96

our heavenly Father, is when a person will receive that sacrifice and repent. Jesus knew no sin during His thirty-three years on earth. He was pure, spotless, and clean from all iniquity. Once the sins of the entire world were placed on Him, He became the sacrificial lamb that took away the sins of the world, *once and for all*. When a person accepts Christ as Lord and Savior, asks for forgiveness of his sins, turns away from his old life and habitual sinning, and surrenders his life to live as Christ, he becomes heir to the kingdom of God. At this point, his sins are as far away from him as the east is from the west.

> He has not dealt with us according to our sins, Nor rewarded us according to our iniquities. For as high as the heavens are above the earth, So great is His loving kindness toward those who fear Him. As far as the east is from the west, So far has He removed our transgressions from us. Just as a father has compassion on his children, So the LORD has compassion on those who fear Him. For He Himself knows our frame; He is mindful that we are but dust.
>
> PSALM 103:10–14 (NASB)

Before Christ's sacrifice, the high priest and the heads of households had to make several types of offerings several times a year to atone for their sins and the sins of their nation. The book of Leviticus gives a detailed account of the different types of offerings that God expected for atonement, obedience, and worship. It was the responsibility of the head of the household to make the altar of sacrifice and prepare and offer the sacrifice to cover the family's sins. Here is a summary of the offerings and their meanings.

The *whole burnt offering* for atonement of sins and dedication of the whole life to God. Only animals, without blemish and washed before the offering, were used for the sin offerings for reconciliation, expression of devotion, and obedience. Bulls, sheep, goats, pigeons, or doves were the animals used for this type of offering, depending on your financial ability. It is not the offering as much as it is the sincerity and sacrifice of the best you have to give. The entire animal was burnt on the altar (Leviticus 1).

The *grain offering* must be with fine flour and symbolized the everyday gift of life from God as it was the staple of their diet. Only a portion of this offering was burned, and the remainder was given to the Levitical priests. The grain had to be mixed with oil and frankincense, and it must be unleavened and a sweet aroma to the LORD. Salt also needed to be added to the offering to remind the Israelites of God. *It is the most holy of the offerings to the LORD made by fire* (Leviticus 2:3).

The *peace offering* was a burnt offering of the fat of the animals, and the remainder was used as a meal. The blood was drained and sprinkled all around the altar by the priests. The offering symbolized fellowship and thanksgiving and was voluntary (Leviticus 3).

The *sin offering* covered unintentional sins against the LORD or, if the priest sins, bringing guilt to the people. This offering would be a young bull without blemish. This sacrifice was made repeatedly, as you could quite imagine, a temporary covering of our sins. This was a sacrifice of repentance in breaking relations with God and endangering the community (Leviticus 4).

Imagine what our land would look like if we were still offering young bulls for every sin! Environmentalists would be in a constant dilemma as to the solutions.

The *guilt offering* was mandatory when a person sinned against another or regarding the Lord's holy things. The sacrifice was a ram without blemish, plus restitution to the one who was wronged, plus an additional 20 percent (Leviticus 5).

As I think about all these sacrifices, I can't imagine how any of us would be able to keep livestock, not to mention the effect on the convictions of our fellow vegans and vegetarians… just think: *unintentional sinning* needed a sacrifice!

Praise God for His wonderful mercy on us that Jesus is the only sacrifice we need to cover intentional and unintentional sins, and we have complete access to Him for thanksgiving and relationship with the Holy God. No grains or animals need to be offered; when God looks at us, He does not see our sins but His Son and His righteousness. I am beyond words when I think of the price Jesus paid for our iniquities, known and unknown. I feel my awareness does not even come close to the depth of truth in this sacrifice. He died for *all men*, for *all time*. All our weaknesses, iniquities, faults, imperfections, condemnations, and offenses to ourselves and others are completely washed away and covered by the blood of Jesus.

"He made Him who knew no sin to be sin on our behalf, so that we might become the righteousness of God in Him" (2 Corinthians 5:21, NASB).

"For what the law was powerless to do in that it was weakened by the flesh, God did by sending His own Son in the likeness of sinful man, as an offering for sin. He thus condemned sin in the flesh" (Romans 8:3, BSB).

"It is because of Him that you are in Christ Jesus, who has become for us wisdom from God: our righteousness, holiness, and redemption" (1 Corinthians 1:30, BSB).

Another important point I would like to make here is that sin does not have partiality with God. All sin carries the same weight in the eyes of God… lying is the same sin as murder. Jesus carries the scars for all sins in thought, word, and deed.

— Chapter 7 —

SATAN IS OUR ENEMY, NOT PEOPLE

#3 TRUTH—SATAN IS NOT EQUAL TO GOD IN POWER OR MAJESTY—HE IS IN OPPOSITION OF GOD AND HIS PURPOSES, BUT DOES NOT THREATEN HIS POWER

> I am the LORD, and there is no other; Besides Me there is no God. I will gird you, though you have not known Me; That men may know from the rising to the setting of the sun That there is no one besides Me. I am the LORD, and there is no other, The One forming light and creating darkness, Causing well-being and creating calamity; I am the LORD who does all these.
>
> ISAIAH 45:5–7 (NASB)

The definition of the word "satan" is translated as "adversary." He is the chief of the fallen angels, and his sole purpose is to wreak havoc on earth and accuse God's people. In the book of Job, he accuses Job's faithfulness due to God's blessings on his life; however, when all the blessings were removed, Job remained faithful.

First Timothy gives us a clue to satan's downfall when he references mankind: "lest being puffed up with pride he fall into the same condemnation as the devil" (1 Timothy 3:6, NKJV).

In the book of Zechariah, in one of his eight visions, satan is referenced as standing at the right hand of Joshua, the high priest, to oppose him. Joshua was standing before the angel of the LORD in filthy garments as a representation of the nation of Israel's sins, and the LORD rebuked satan. "And the LORD said to Satan, 'The LORD rebuke you, Satan! The LORD who has chosen Jerusalem rebuke you!" (Zechariah 3:2, NKJV).

The New Testament mentions satan over thirty-five times with many different names, such as tempter, ruler of demons, evil one, enemy, the father of lies, murderer, ruler of this world, and the prince of the power of the air, to name a few. Apostle Paul warned the Corinthians that he might appear as an "angel

103

of light." Regardless of the temptations that satan may dangle in front of man, he does not have the power to coerce a person to sin. Man's free will decides that. We are told, in the book of James, "Submit therefore to God. Resist the devil and he will flee from you" (James 4:7, NASB). Satan ultimately has no power over us, nor do his demons. They have already been judged and defeated by the death and resurrection of Jesus Christ. We have the armor of God to protect us and the name of Jesus to cause him to flee. The greatest defense against satan is the Word of God.

🌿 *Know God's Word, and you will never be under deception.* 🌿

The greatest example of this is recorded in the Gospels when satan tries to deceive and tempt Christ in the wilderness. Jesus uses only Scripture to fight him, quietly and powerfully. Jesus is hungry and tired after spending forty days in the wilderness after his baptism, and satan appears to Him three times.

In the Gospel of Matthew, immediately after John the Baptist baptized Jesus, God's voice erupted from heaven announcing that this is His Beloved Son in whom He is pleased, and we are told that Jesus was led by the Holy Spirit into the wilderness. He fasted for forty days and nights, and the tempter came to Him and tried to convince Jesus to sin.

104

First temptation. "If You are the Son of God, command that these stones become bread" (Matthew 4:3, NASB). Jesus responds, "Man shall not live on Bread alone, but on every word that proceeds out of the mouth of God" (Matthew 4:4, NASB).

Second temptation. The devil takes Jesus above the holy city on the pinnacle of the temple and says, "If You are the Son of God, throw Yourself down" (Matthew 4:6, NASB), and then satan quotes the scriptures that state, "It is written, 'He will command His angels concerning You;' and 'On their hands they will bear You up So that You will not strike Your foot against a stone'" (Matthew 4:6, NASB). Jesus responds—"On the other hand, it is written, 'You shall not put the LORD Your God to the test'" (Matthew 4:7, NASB).

Final temptation. The devil takes Jesus to a very high mountain and shows Him all the kingdoms of the world and their glory and tells Jesus he would give Him all these things if He would bow down and worship him. Then Jesus said to him, "Go away, Satan! For it is written: 'You shall worship the LORD your God, and serve Him only'" (Matthew 4:10, NASB).

Satan left Jesus, and angels appeared and ministered to our Savior. If satan is so bold, brazen, and proud as to try to tempt the Son of God, how much more should we be prepared to be tempted? He failed because he has no power other than to twist words and disguise truth with lies. Once again, satan's only goal is to move God's people away from worshipping God to bowing before him. Given that he has no power and all you need to do is to rebuke him, he is equivalent to a *no-see-um* (annoying biting bugs native to Florida). Or maybe it is what the *no-see-um* feeds on, which I am not sure that anybody knows what it might be.

#4 TRUTH—WE ARE FIGHTING AGAINST POWERS, PRINCIPALITIES, AND EVIL, NOT PEOPLE

We do not fight with people but with the powers, principalities, and evil that exert influence in this world. Satan, the father of lies, uses his lies and deceptions to cause chaos in our world.

> You are of your father the devil, and you want to do the desires of your father. He was a murderer from the beginning, and does not stand in the truth because there is no truth in him. Whenever he speaks a lie, he speaks from his own nature, for he is a liar and the father of lies.
>
> JOHN 8:44 (NASB)

106

Satan uses hatred, division, and lofty ideas to make people disagree and distance themselves from each other. If we can stop and call him out, humble ourselves, and pray, God will hear our prayer and heal our land. When we entertain arguments and dispute theories, we feed evil. There is absolutely nothing that happens under the sun that is not provincially ordained by God. He takes the choices that are made by mankind and turns them into good for those who love Him and are called according to His purpose. He allows people to make a choice by their free will, but when that free will collides with the path of one of His children, he will use it for His good. Sometimes, the child of God must walk through the situation; sometimes, they must walk around it; and sometimes, they are lifted above it and soar like an eagle. Whatever the outcome, we need to trust that God's hand is in it, and no weapon formed against us shall prosper, and every tongue that rises up against us shall be cast down in the mighty name of Jesus. There are also times when God will remove people from you for your good because He loves you and is trying to protect you from harm. Keep in mind that people have free will and are always evolving. At times, they evolve in the wrong direction, and God puts a hedge of protection around us. We may not understand the separation;

we may not have caused the separation, but nonetheless, it has occurred.

I understand we are to trust God in all things, always, and we hear sayings like, "The battle belongs to the Lord; it is not our battle." This is very true. Our faith should always be in God, but don't lose sight of our enemy that shows up at our lowest point. Sometimes we need to be giant slayers and think in terms of a wartime strategy against our enemy. Remember, the subtle undercurrent of deception is like a tsunami: it starts deep below the water as a thin crack and grows, splits, and creates an underwater typhoon that erupts to the surface and overtakes the land, destroying relationships that never recover. We are at war against our enemy daily, and that enemy is satan! We have a part in slaying our giants, and God prepared us for our daily battle by instructing us,

> Finally, be strong in the Lord and in the strength of his might. Put on the whole armor of God, that you may be able to stand against the schemes of the devil. For we do not wrestle against flesh and blood, but against the rulers, against the authorities, against the cosmic powers over this present darkness, against the spiritual forces of

108

evil in the heavenly places. Therefore take up the whole armor of God, that you may be able to withstand in the evil day, and having done all, to stand firm. Stand therefore, having fastened on the belt of truth, and having put on the breastplate of righteousness, and, as shoes for your feet, having put on the readiness given by the gospel of peace. In all circumstances take up the shield of faith, with which you can extinguish all the flaming darts of the evil one; and take the helmet of salvation, and the sword of the Spirit, which is the word of God, praying at all times in the Spirit, with all prayer and supplication. To that end, keep alert with all perseverance, making supplication for all the saints.[12]

EPHESIANS 6:10–18 (ESV)

Satan has never changed his original plan of attack against God and His kingdom and mankind. Before God created man, earth, and the heavens, only the angels existed with Him and Jesus. How long was this period? We are not privy to that in the Scriptures. I imagine it was not important for us to know this in God's plan, or He would have told us. Satan was called Lucifer,

12   "Ephesians 6:10–18 ESV," Bible Gateway, accessed November 17, 2023, https://www.biblegateway.com/passage/?search=Ephesians%206%3A10%E2%80%9318%20&version=ESV.

and he was a beautiful angel, a worshipper, equal in rank to Michael, Gabriel, and Uriel, the archangels.

I am supposing that God did not discuss His plan to create man, earth, and the heavens with any of the angels. I further suppose that this is when Lucifer became angry with God and decided to plan his rebellion. God poured His love, time, and creativity into His new creation. Making Adam and Eve in His image and giving them free will, unlike the angels who are ministering spirits and can only do what God orders them to do. This includes the mighty archangels. They do not act on their own… they wait on the Father to give them orders, send them with announcements, or send them to intervene as protectors, but never interfere with free will. They have positions; some are worshipers, some are warriors, some are guardians, and some protect and surround the throne of God day and night. They are content and honored to be in the position and presence of God for eternity.

When did God let the angels know of His plan? I cannot say, but His creation of mankind immediately threatened Lucifer, and he set out to prove to God that mankind was not worth His time nor love and that mankind would disappoint, disobey, disrespect, disregard, and destroy God's intentions of creating a relationship with mankind as a family. Remember the account of Job… it is the only time God fully shared the length that satan would go to prove his point against mankind; however, I believe that one story is the epitome of the constant accusations brought against us that satan uses to this very day. Lucifer rebelled and took one-third of the angels with him and continues today to convince God that mankind was the worst thing ever created. I imagine God reminds satan of Job constantly, as a reminder of his failed efforts, and smiles lovingly down on mankind as we glorify Him in the good times as well as the devastating times, as Job did.

(Do we disappoint God? Yes, but He views us through the lens of the righteousness of Jesus… That is the wonder of the death and resurrection.)

Banished to earth, satan is free to roam like a roaring lion, wreaking havoc among mankind using lies and deception, giving knowledge of depravity, murder, witchcraft, mind washing, control, oppression and hunger, and all lofty ideas that are opposite of goodness. He continues to strive to remove God and His ways for the minds and hearts of mankind by using hatred and division as the catalyst of controversy. So, when we fight amongst each other, we are not fighting the person, situation, or circumstance, but we are battling the adversary of all times and his demons. Their punishment is sealed, waiting for the day God imposes it. Satan continues to plan attacks and counterattacks against mankind to win the battle as a spoiled child trying to get out of the judgment that is already set in God's time.

When you are in the middle of trauma and grief, weakened by heartbreak, pain, and fear, satan will use that very situation to make you hate God, to blame Him for the death, the separation, the hurt that was inflected, the abandonment, to bring condemnation to you. Do not allow him to have a foothold! Stand firm in your mess, in your tears, in your brokenness, and use the words Jesus used in the wilderness, "Go away, Satan! For it is written: 'You shall worship the LORD your God, and serve Him only'" (Matthew 4:10, NASB).

— *Chapter 8* —

PRAYER AND OUR POSTURE

#5 TRUTH—PRAYER ALWAYS
PRECEDES PEACE AND RESTORATION

Relationships are broken in families, between husbands and wives, parents and children, siblings, grandparents and children, in-laws, extended families, work environments, and friendships. Every relationship can suffer a break that is sometimes on purpose or so many times unintentional, but it is like a ship in the night without a light heading toward a rocky shore. It just comes out of the blue and slams right into you. Obviously, I am talking from personal experience. In the last decade, I have been overtaken by situations that I never would have expected in my lifetime. Some are resolved quickly; for others, it takes years or maybe never. At times, refer back to the "two chairs;" just talking to the person when not present is what God intends you to do. The high road is the road best taken, and that road is a *path of prayer, more prayer, much prayer, and continued prayer.* There is so much to learn and say about prayer; in fact, there are so many books on prayer by great prayer warriors who have walked this earth that it could take a lifetime to read them all.

One key element that I have learned by reading many of these books—along with my prayers (answered and yet to be answered) and Jesus's teaching on prayer—is that in any conflict, God loves all the people involved equally. He does not take sides or wait for us to realize our part, intentionally or unintentionally, in the severed relationship to resume His relationship with us. He does not miss a beat in His one-on-one love with us. He does not join in our rationale over the disagreement or tell us, "It is not your fault; it's the other person's." Nothing changes in His love for you or the other party. He does not join you in the blame game or sympathize with your woes. He loves equally and unconditionally and deals with each of us at the heart level. He remains the same loving Savior to all, always, without condemnation to either party. Isn't that amazing?

He empathizes with everyone because His wisdom and grace are amazing. We, on the other hand, in our head, out loud, or to a sympathetic ear, are defending our actions and justifying our position and reasons; He just listens without comment to our ramblings. When He does speak, it is not, "Well, I see your point; you are definitely right, and they are clearly wrong; you have every right to feel that way." *No*, that will never happen! It cannot happen! He will judge, but you will never know His judgment unless He wants you to. Time will pass, and all parties will continue to be blessed and guided regardless of the fallout. The divine order of each life will not hinge on your disagreement or be threatened by it. God shows no partiality over His children, and thankfully so! Your sin will be before you, and that is what He will deal with. The sin of unforgiveness, pride, anger, malice, ill will, keeping of wrongs, no matter the circumstance. The Samaritan woman at the well was told by Jesus, in John 4:15–18 (NASB),

"Go, call your husband and come here." The woman answered and said to Him, "I have no husband." Jesus said to her, "You have correctly said, 'I have no husband'; for you have had five husbands, and the one whom you now have is not your husband; this which you have said is true.

115

He didn't say, "Poor dear, I know how hard life has been, a Samaritan Woman who does not know the law... You didn't have a choice but to act the way you did; you needed to survive; all the other women have men to take care of them. It is a harsh world... you were forced into that life."

The prostitute was not placated about her choices. Jesus got straight to the heart of the matter... His relationship with her... her purity to have the relationship with Him... His gift of living water, not withheld. So, when we are in a broken relationship, He will deal with our hearts, not the other person or persons. Jesus does not take a side in any matter between men, He offers forgiveness, grace, and love, and we need only accept it. Follow His directions on how to mend the broken relationship. Sometimes, it calls for humility and asks for forgiveness from the person, sometimes silent forgiveness, sometimes talking to a "chair." It will be His direction, not your decision, that should be followed, nothing but trust and waiting. But by no means think that He will stop His relationship with the other person just because you have stopped yours! We are all equal and equally cared for and loved each day by our Lord for all eternity!

I began thinking about all this due to an estrangement I had with my son for a period and how life progressed for both of us during that time, with continued blessings, joys, and ongoing daily life. Even though I could camp on the scripture that he should have honored me because I was his mother and the consequences of not doing that, *I realized* in my heartfelt prayers for him that those prayers didn't make God take care of him; it just showed God a mother's heart of love and longing to be in a restored relationship, and God did.

God does not need our prayers to move, He is love and watches over all His children equally! He loves my son more than I do, and no weapon formed against him shall prosper, and every tongue that revolts against him shall be cast down, even if it would be my own. God delights in seeing our hearts soften, pliable, and a mirror of Jesus, sacrificing our own desires, or in most cases, the need to be right in our own eyes. When we enter into prayer for another person, our compassion takes over our self-righteousness, and God responds! My unselfish prayers, my thanks for restoration, and my waiting for God to intervene brought the solution and the peace. Is this what each disagreement, estrangement, and conflict needs to bring resolution? I honestly believe so with every fiber of my being!

117

How do we, in our grief, brokenness, and heartache, place our prayers at the feet of Jesus until God brings resolution without interfering? It is not easy; we think if we call, text, cry, or say something so profound, we will change the situation. That is the furthest from the truth, and many times, the interference prolongs the resolution. Our view is like looking at the back of a cross stitch: strings going every which way, no pattern, just a messy mess! But turn it over and you'll find such beauty; that is God's view: all the colors are exactly where they belong, every prayer in its own box perfectly, put together.

🌿 *Prayer always precedes peace and restoration!* 🌿

A public conflict that recently occurred sheds further light on this understanding. Two well-known, faithful Christians had a word war over social media recently, unfortunately, for all the world to see. Did each of us take sides secretly or publicly, find scriptures to back up our viewpoint, and feel sure God would see it that same way? Many of us, *yes!*

I imagine God's response to be, "I am so fond of those two." God will not treat one less than the other; stop loving one less than the other. He will speak in a quiet, gentle voice

His commands to love one another, to forgive one another, to remember the price His Son paid for their eternity. The Holy Spirit will remind them that they are the righteousness of God in Christ Jesus. His sovereignty will reign over the situation, and neither will lose His tender loving-kindness.

❧ Our opinions, reasons, and theories do not move God ❧

The takeaway from this is simply this: in all things, seek God's perspective, pray, and allow Him to show you the way. I know there is much pain in a relationship that has been ripped apart; the agony it brings makes it hard to breathe. The tears are endless and frequent, and certain times of the year bring further despair, so I am not minimizing the pain as you navigate through it; I am just trying to give you direction and hope to guide you. Our objections, opinions, and disagreements do not move God, but that is not Him being mean; it is His divine plan for you and the other person. We cannot fathom the reasons, but it does not mean God is wrong or unjust; it is the fact that He is *just*, and He does what He does. If He were unjust, we would never be able to atone for all our sins. Think back to the sacrifices; could you imagine visiting a priest daily to bring an animal to burn on an altar? A way was made beyond our imagination to cover our sins and reconcile us back to God without daily offerings. One gift of one sacrifice, one time, for all eternity.

One of the greatest pastors and faithful men of God of all times passed recently (2023) at the age of ninety, Dr. Charles Stanley. In one of his last interviews, he was asked, "What do you want people to understand the most about or live by in their Christian walk?" (paraphrased). Dr. Stanley states, "Obey God and leave all the consequences to Him."[13] I like to insert the word "trust" in that quote. So, no matter what the circumstance, trauma, grief, or brokenness, put it at the feet of Jesus, and don't pick it up. Obey and trust that He will make a way, bring peace, bring truth, bring light, and bring PTLL (praise the Lord living).

#6 TRUTH—DECREASE SO THAT HE INCREASES

As death is part of life, and there is no situation that Jesus did not address in the thirty-three years He walked the earth, I believe that our moving forward in love, joy, happiness, generosity, and contentment is required of us even when dealing with grief. Do we still hurt? Yes, but we should be thankful

---

13   "Life Principle 2: A Life of Obedience," In Touch Ministries, accessed November 17, 2023, https://www.intouch.org/index.php/watch/sermons/life-principle-2-a-life-of-obedience.

every morning for the new day that we have been given and for the responsibility we have to those who still count on us each day! You still have purpose; seek it, run after it, and immerse yourself into finding it.

You may not be at the point to accept this; you may throw this book across the room in anger, but go pick it up! It is important for me to continue encouraging you and speaking from a place of healing and victory over your grief, even if you are not. I know you will get there!

❧ Faith always precedes feelings and emotions ❧

Replace your anger, hurt, and grieving with generosity to others and God's will for your life. There are two roads you can travel. One is lonely, bitter, self-absorbed, and angry. *The other is filled with light and love, and it is generous, giving, peaceful, and happy.*

John the Baptist teaches us about decreasing and stepping aside so that Jesus can increase in His ministry. I would say that John's actions were not only his duty under God's will but his gracious consent. He led the way for a greater cause. John

121

was a cousin to Jesus and spent many years in the wilderness preaching and proclaiming the coming of Jesus and baptizing hundreds. When the time was appointed for Jesus to be baptized and receive the Holy Spirit, He found John and was baptized by him. There was a point in time before John was thrown in prison and beheaded, when Jesus was baptizing His disciples and others, and some approached John,

> And they came to John and said to him, "Rabbi, He who was with you beyond the Jordan, to whom you have testified, behold, He is baptizing and all are coming to Him." John answered and said, "A man can receive nothing unless it has been given him from heaven. You yourselves are my witnesses that I said, 'I am not the Christ,' but, 'I have been sent ahead of Him.' He who has the bride is the bridegroom; but the friend of the bridegroom, who stands and hears him, rejoices greatly because of the bridegroom's voice. So this joy of mine has been made full. He must increase, but I must decrease.
>
> JOHN 3:26–30 (NASB)

Grace is given to you by someone; graciousness is your gift to the world. Imagine a world where every human being would encourage and help others get their wants and needs met before their own. Everything a person does is geared toward the betterment of another. That is the way God's relationship with us is. His every thought, action, teaching, and revelation is for our betterment. Therefore, that is our example of how we should be toward others so that we mirror God to the world. As we decrease our own wants, desires, and self-promotion and replace them with God's love, we become imitators of Him, and ultimately, He increases. It is not us anymore, but Christ who lives in us.

> Since we have gifts that differ according to the grace given to us, each of us is to exercise them accordingly: if prophecy, according to the proportion of his faith; if service, in his serving; or he who teaches, in his teaching; or he who exhorts, in his exhortation; he who gives, with liberality; he who leads, with diligence; he who shows mercy, with cheerfulness.
>
> Let love be without hypocrisy. Abhor what is evil; cling to what is good. Be devoted to one another in brotherly love; give preference to one another

in honor; not lagging behind in diligence, fervent in spirit, serving the Lord; rejoicing in hope, persevering in tribulation, devoted to prayer, contributing to the needs of the saints, practicing hospitality.

Bless those who persecute you; bless and do not curse. Rejoice with those who rejoice, and weep with those who weep. Be of the same mind toward one another; do not be haughty in mind, but associate with the lowly. Do not be wise in your own estimation. Never pay back evil for evil to anyone. Respect what is right in the sight of all men. If possible, so far as it depends on you, be at peace with all men. Never take your own revenge, beloved, but leave room for the wrath of God, for it is written, "Vengeance is Mine, I will repay," says the Lord. "But if your enemy is hungry, feed him, and if he is thirsty, give him a drink; for in so doing you will heap burning coals on his head." Do not be overcome by evil, but overcome evil with good.

ROMANS 12:6–21 (NASB)

This is the graciousness that we should give because it is the grace we receive. The above scripture is a vivid picture of the gift of graciousness. No matter what your gift, resources, or

124

sphere of influence, we should be walking out Romans 12:6–21 in our everyday life. Is this accomplished with ease, or will it take till twenty, thirty, forty, fifty, or even sixty years of age? Do you see glimpses of it and wish it would happen more often? Are you ready to sacrifice yourself not in self-promotion or self-improvement but in *decreasing so that Christ can increase?*

The reality is a conscious effort where we view every encounter, conversation, connection, and interaction at home, at work, and in our world as a gift that you receive on Christmas morning or your birthday. Expectation, wonder, joy, and deeper understanding should be your stance. Never anticipating monotony but enjoying the journey, whether it is a brief encounter with a person or a life-long relationship.

It is the long, winding road of life that God predetermined for you to walk; He placed every encounter along that path, and you are a farmer on that path. You are sowing seeds and reaping a harvest. Charles Stanley had the following to say: "Every farmer understands the meaning of this principle: We reap what we sow, more than we sow, and later than we sow."[14]

---

14   "Life Principle 6: The Principle of Sowing and Reaping," In Touch Ministries, accessed November 17, 2023, https://www.intouch.org/watch/sermons/life-principle-6-the-principle-of-sowing-and-reaping.

As Christians, we are like farmers, sowing seeds throughout life and allowing the Holy Spirit to seal, convict, and teach the receiver of the seeds.

In a discussion with my granddaughter about an upcoming trip where she would be in a car for eight hours, she said, *"I am looking forward to the destination but not the journey, even though I know that I am supposed to enjoy the journey."* She was ten at the time and already understood this concept much earlier than I did; therefore, she will probably sow more seeds and enjoy much more on her life journey. Now, at fourteen, she says, *"What you give power to is what holds the power."* It is pretty profound if you ask me.

What seeds are you leaving along your journey? Is the path beaten down and ripped apart? Is it a vast barrenness unable for the seeds you sow to root due to neglect? *Or* are there sporadic splashes of color with no consistency? *Or* is your path, as you look back, lush, strong, colorful, with towering fruit-bearing trees and flowers always in bloom?

In Jesus' ministry and teachings, He describes how seeds should be sown and the effect, or lack of effect, they can have. I believe that this analogy is a wise lesson on the seeds we

126

sow and the footprints we leave as we interact with our world, our sphere of influence, and with our children, family, friends, coworkers, and strangers.

Jesus says that some seeds fell beside the road, no soil or water, and the birds and squirrels, those rascal creatures, came and stole them. These are the words we speak haphazardly, harsh words, not caring where they land on the person. These seeds are also the words we hear that God wants us to understand to enrich our lives, but satan comes and snatches them away because there is no foundation, leaving a vast path of barrenness in our hearts and our lives.

Some seeds fall in rocky places with some soil; they spring up, but the heat of the day scorches them, and they wither away, unable to take root. These are our relationships that are shallow; we are unable to give beyond the surface. We do not take the time to nurture and flitter here and there as the mood or emotions take us. We are temporal in our thinking about the momentary comfort or feeling we desire. When we receive God's Word, we are immediately overcome with joy, but because there is no root, the joy falls away quickly when difficult circumstances arise. We are not grounded in the Word of God and allow the ideas and theories of the world to dictate our lives. It becomes very easy for satan to snatch away the newfound joy. We neglect to nurture the Word of God in our lives, to meditate on His Word, and shut out the noise of the world.

The book of Matthew 13 teaches us about where seeds fall and the results. Sometimes seeds fall among thorns, and they are choked and unable to grow. These are representative of those who hear the Word of God but allow the idols of the world to choke out the good seeds and stop them from bearing fruit. Worry about money and earthly possessions overtake us, causing us to be selfish in giving of ourselves and our resources. We will help but pull back when we feel our resources or time is draining; our lives have sporadic splashes of color but no consistency, and the thorns are among the flowers, hindering them from flourishing.

Some seeds fall on rich, good soil, yielding a large crop. These are those who hear, understand, and nurture the Word of God. They seek to know God more intimately each day; they cultivate relationships, walk in peace with all men, and become imitators of God, made in His image, spreading love, and giving of themselves without holding back. They are bearing fruit

128

and leaving a legacy for future generations that is lush, strong, colorful, towering, fruit-bearing trees and flowers always in bloom.

The seeds we sow as we walk through life can affect future generations of our families in positive ways that will be full of favor and blessings or in negative ways that can have destruction at every turn. We can break generational curses or perpetuate them. We need to be intentional in our actions and decisions, showing our children, family, and friends the importance of choosing God's precepts, laws, teachings, and wisdom as opposed to the ideals, theories, teachings, and passing trends of the world. Knowing truths versus deceptions is the foundation of a life that will produce a healthy crop that can be harvested many times over.

Are you sowing truth or deception in your life?

We reap what we sow, greater than we sow and later than we sow.[15]

---

15 "Life Principle 6: The Principle of Sowing and Reaping," In Touch Ministries, accessed November 17, 2023, https://www.intouch.org/watch/sermons/life-principle-6-the-principle-of-sowing-and-reaping.

#7 TRUTH—BEING CLAY
IN THE HANDS FOR THE POTTER

At birth, we are pure and innocent, with no impressions, imperfections, soul ties, memories, or visible personalities. We are pliable at the hands of our parents and soak up learning like a sponge. Spiritually, we are also pliable in the Hands of God when we accept Him into our life. Once that occurs, we are set apart, sealed by the Holy Spirit, a piece of clay on the self, amongst others, not distinguishable yet. On occasion, God will take us down to see if we are ready to fully become putty in His hands. To be shifted, shaped, squashed, and shifted again until we form the perfect piece of pottery. What stops this process is our will to be rulers of our own lives, mostly to our own demise.

Some of us remain on this shelf until we become hopeless and helpless when we are tired of doing things in our own strength and have made a mess of things. We begin to wonder about the purpose of life and our place in it. God has tried to shape us, but we are resistant and need more time on the shelf despite the hard times, struggles, defeat, and even some disasters due to our stubborn nature, pride, or mostly satan's deception.

Or maybe we are the ones who have sat in church all our lives, heard all about God, and still have no clue who or what He is in our lives. No heart knowledge, no sensitivity to the Holy Spirit, just head knowledge. Eventually, all of us come to a crisis of belief and either surrender totally to God's will or remain stubborn and stay on the shelf. We are secure in our passage to heaven through salvation but never experience the kingdom of God on earth in our lives. The Lord's Prayer states, "Thy kingdom come, thy will be done on earth, as it is in heaven."

When we don't move toward surrender, we don't experience the pure joy of living and the awe of watching God do miraculous things in our lives and those around us. We miss His blessings and settle for what we can do for ourselves with our own abilities.

A life without the power and presence of God is guaranteed to be a life full of unrest and turmoil.

Then there are those of us who long to be on the potter's wheel, off the shelf where the journey begins. You are ready to totally surrender and make Jesus Lord of your life, and He begins the molding and shaping according to His design and purpose. You are easy and willing to be on God's wheel for a very long time. This is where you not only deal with your sins but repent. Your character begins to change because the Lord is building you up. You are squished, squashed, stretched; you deal with your inner self, your baggage, your habits, and family issues. You are learning His Word, and you are attending church regularly, giving of your time, resources, and talents joyfully. You are trying to figure out who God is in your life; you begin to be formed into a new creature in Christ. This is where your faith begins to grow as God shows you how to be selfless and totally dependent on Him. Faith growing means going through the valley and over mountains, some small and some exceptionally large, and trusting the Lord till you get to the other side. Some of us go around the same mountains till we move them or conquer them.

> But the vessel that he was making of clay was spoiled in the hand of the potter; so he remade it into another vessel, as it pleased the potter to make. Then the word of the LORD came to me saying, "Can I not, O house of Israel, deal with you as this potter does?" declares the LORD. "Behold, like the clay in the potter's hand, so are you in

My hand, O house of Israel [Bride of Christ]. At one moment I might speak concerning a nation or concerning a kingdom to uproot, to pull down, or to destroy it; if that nation against which I have spoken turns from its evil, I will relent concerning the calamity I planned to bring on it. Or at another moment I might speak concerning a nation or concerning a kingdom to build up or to plant it; if it does evil in My sight by not obeying My voice, then I will think better of the good with which I had promised to bless it."

JEREMIAH 18:4–10 (NASB)

#8 TRUTH—LIGHT HAS NO FELLOWSHIP WITH DARKNESS

This truth is based on 2 Corinthians 6:14, where Paul tells us that righteousness and lawlessness have no partnership and that light and darkness are not in fellowship. Believers and unbelievers have nothing in common, as Christ and satan have nothing in common. Either a person has accepted Jesus as Savior and King, or they have not; it is black and white, no gray area, no partway to salvation. Paul further goes on to talk about having idols in our lives. Idols can be anything

133

that stands in the way or hinders our relationship with Christ. Unlike the distinction of believing or accepting Christ as Lord, many Christians still hold on to idols in their life that limit their growth and freedom of the Holy Spirit fully working in their lives. Idols can be career, money, power, materials, or even love of a person over the love of God. Idols can also be our self-image or self-sufficiency, which is sometimes harder to give up.

As we learn to walk further with God, he will begin to remove idols from our lives, and those of us who are shown an area that God considers an idol will either give it up or God may allow things to happen so that we see He is all the sufficiency we need, until we give it up. God teaches many some of the same lessons, but our will determines how many times we must go around the same mountain till we get it.

For example, if money is the idol, He may allow some things to hit your bank account to show you that no matter what the balance, He will provide for you as He does the birds of the air. It isn't that He does not want us to prosper; in fact, He would like us to be very prosperous, but if you love money more than you love Him, you will be taught to let go and let God provide.

In my experience, I have seen Christians struggle more with

134

getting love and attention from their spouse, self-image, and self-worth than money and resources. Those are emotional needs that run deep due to many factors, including the environment we grew up in. Many of us deal with childhood memories of not having parents around, being raised by a single parent, or not feeling loved and secure because parents were too busy working out their own issues and challenges. For whatever reason, a lack of emotional needs being met, I believe, is the hardest to overcome.

Women fall under the need to get their husbands to fulfill many emotional wounds that *only* God can. Yet, they will keep looking to their husband to fill the void, and when the husband is unable or unwilling, the idol becomes the *obsession of their husband's approval.* It ruins marriages because too many expectations are put on the husband, and he is most often unaware of this and unable to meet them. In the meanwhile, he is trying to learn how to be the man God wants him to be and cannot give more than God is already shaking up in his own life.

Or the husband uses the spouse's obsessive need for approval to make himself feel powerful and abuses that power.

This leads to an extremely unhealthy and abusive relationship of dependency and control. These examples are not what God intended a marriage to be.

Self-image and self-worth can be big enemies in the way we view our past, present, and future. We carry our unsolved issues from childhood and teenage years into adulthood and marriage. Now, with more responsibility to our spouse and children, we may be unable to sort them out. Insecurities that we have not worked through can cause us to be adults who fall back to past comforts that help us cope. Overeating, overdrinking, prescription drugs, street drugs, pornography, recklessness, promiscuity, or any other distraction that turns our focus away from our issue. Most often, what we think is the solution becomes the bigger problem that feeds our lack of worth or physical image. When darkness from our past overtakes our present and future, the lie that our identity is found in our relationship with anyone other than Christ leads to unresolved self-image and worth. This foundation then leads to a personality that is motivated by a codependent personality. The truth is that you are only complete in Christ.

See to it that no one takes you captive through philosophy and empty deception, according to the tradition of men, according to the elementary principles of the world, rather than according to Christ. For in Him all the fullness of Deity dwells in bodily form, and in Him you have been made complete, and He is the head over all rule and authority.

COLOSSIANS 2:8–10 (NASB)

Therefore if you have been raised up with Christ, keep seeking the things above, where Christ is, seated at the right hand of God. Set your mind on the things above, not on the things that are on earth…When Christ, who is our life, is revealed, then you also will be revealed with Him in glory.

COLOSSIANS 3:1–2, 4 (NASB)

#9 TRUTH—JESUS IS THE WAY, THE TRUTH, AND THE LIFE FOR EVERYONE

Codependent people have a need to rescue, fix, and help others who usually do not want their help to begin with. It is their need to gain love or be a rescuer to cover their own insecurities

137

and to give themselves purpose and meaning. Codependents do not see things accurately, have no boundaries, or have unhealthy boundaries. The act of codependency becomes the idol in your life. The need to fix someone else keeps your eye off one's-self and not on your Creator. Energy is wasted on fixing a person that you are not responsible for fixing. God is the potter for every human being, and Jesus directs the way, shines His light on the truth, and gives eternal life. Denial of one's inabilities keeps you stuck on the big X of life, unable to see the truth. "He who conceals his transgressions will not prosper, But he who confesses and forsakes them will find compassion" (Proverbs 28:13, NASB).[16]

As we have been discussing, truth is light, and deception is darkness. Facing the truth and bringing it into the light moves us away from deception. Only our heavenly Father can teach, protect, and assure us of this journey in our lives once we willingly give Him control. Whatever our past, God can restore our minds, hearts, and spirits. Through the sacrifice of Jesus on the cross, we become whole. We must believe this and develop an accurate understanding of who God is. Our relationship

---

16   "Proverbs 28 (NASB95)," Blue Letter Bible, accessed November 17, 2023, https://www.blueletterbible.org/nasb95/pro/28/13/s_656013.

with our parents or those who were responsible for raising us most likely shaped our viewpoint of God. Look at the attributes below and think about which ones best describe the parent or guardian you had growing up.

1. Gentle, loving, kind, intimate, caring, supportive, interested, gracious, wise, sensitive, encouraging, strong, just, good, trustworthy, holy, joyful.

2. Harsh, stern, disapproving, distant, angry, demanding, discipliner, harsh, impatient, unpredictable, passive, unreasonable.

Now, think about your view of God using the above descriptions. If your answers are mostly from the second group, your view of God is very tainted. As you have grown, you might have gained "head knowledge" that God is love and goodness because you have been told this, but is it rooted in your heart? Your experiences and feelings cannot back it up. The actions and behaviors of codependent people stem from and are rooted in feelings and experiences, not exactly our head knowledge. The seeds planted about the character and attributes of God have no strong roots because we did not have the example of love and goodness.

Once we truly admit to ourselves our view of God, we can begin healing the wounds of the past and rewrite the future. Meditate on Psalm 139 to see a wonderful picture of God's Majesty and power!

> O LORD, You have searched me and known me. You know when I sit down and when I rise up; You understand my thought from afar. You scrutinize my path and my lying down and are intimately acquainted with all my ways. Even before there is a word on my tongue, Behold, O LORD, You know it all. You have enclosed me behind and before And laid Your hand upon me. Such knowledge is too wonderful for me; It is too high, I cannot attain to it.
>
> Where can I go from Your Spirit? Or where can I flee from Your presence? If I ascend to heaven, You are there; If I make my bed in Sheol, behold, You are there. If I take the wings of the dawn, If I dwell in the remotest part of the sea, Even there Your hand will lead me, And Your right hand will lay hold of me. If I say, "Surely the darkness will overwhelm me, And the light around me will be night," Even the darkness is not dark to You, And the night is as bright as the day. Darkness and light are alike to You.

For You formed my inward parts; You wove me in my mother's womb.

I will give thanks to You, for I am fearfully and wonderfully made; Wonderful are Your works, And my soul knows it very well. My frame was not hidden from You, When I was made in secret, And skillfully wrought in the depths of the earth; Your eyes have seen my unformed substance; And in Your book were all written The days that were ordained for me, When as yet there was not one of them.

How precious also are Your thoughts to me, O God! How vast is the sum of them! If I should count them, they would outnumber the sand. When I awake, I am still with You.

O that You would slay the wicked, O God; Depart from me, therefore, men of bloodshed. For they speak against You wickedly, And Your enemies take Your name in vain. Do I not hate those who hate You, O LORD? And do I not loathe those who rise up against You? I hate them with the utmost hatred; They have become my enemies.

Search me, O God, and know my heart; Try me and know my anxious thoughts; And see if there be any hurtful way in me, And lead me in the everlasting way.

PSALM 139 (NASB)

Once a person realizes that every individual is accountable to God, precious to God, and powerless to fix others, they can relax and focus on God's relationship with themselves and His plan for their lives. God will heal and restore your mind and remove false beliefs that have ruled and deceived you. Our surrender to God, allowing Him to take control of us and those around us, is the start of true freedom. The world tells us that our worth and significance are determined by what we do, how we dress, what we possess, or what others think about us. The standards of the world become our gauge and our goals. The world's values are the opposite of God's, and His opinion is the only one that truly matters.

He does not view us as failures—*I am forgiven and pleasing to Him.*

He does not reject us—*I am unconditionally accepted.*

He does not need a reason to love us—*I am deeply loved unconditionally.*

He does not condemn us—*I am made brand new and complete in Christ.*

These thoughts might take time and many falls to make them

- PRAYER AND OUR POSTURE -

take root in your heart! Let go of yourself, fellowship daily with God, and let Him work in you. Surrender every situation into His hands and trust His guidance, provision, and sovereignty.

❧ *Give GRACE and SPACE to yourself—He does.* ❧

#10 TRUTH—WORLDLY WAYS ARE ANTI-CHRIST

This is the final and possibly the most important truth in light of the time we are currently living in (December 2023).

Theories, ideas, teachings, values, and morals that are steeped in the world's traditions are always anti-Christ; in other words, they go against His teachings, His commandments, His wisdom, and His character.

Such as the following:

While the world says, "You deserve that promotion, no matter what you need to do to get it, you deserve it!" Scripture says not to grow weary of doing good, to do everything unto the Lord, and that He will reward you.

While the world says, "Do not worry. If your marriage does not work out, you can always get a divorce; everyone does," Scripture states,

And he left there and went to the region of Judea and beyond the Jordan, and crowds gathered to him again. And again, as was his custom, he taught them.

And Pharisees came up and in order to test him asked, "Is it lawful for a man to divorce his wife?" He answered them, "What did Moses command you?" They said, "Moses allowed a man to write a certificate of divorce and to send her away." And Jesus said to them, "Because of your hardness of heart he wrote you this commandment. But from the beginning of creation, 'God made them male and female.' 'Therefore a man shall leave his father and mother and hold fast to his wife, and the two shall become one flesh.' So they are no longer two but one flesh. What therefore God has joined together, let not man separate."

And in the house the disciples asked him again about this matter. And he said to them, "Whoever divorces his wife and marries another commits adultery against her, and if she divorces her husband and marries another, she commits adultery."[17]

MARK 10:1–12 (ESV)

---

[17]   "Mark 10 (ESV)," Blue Letter Bible, accessed November 17, 2023, https://www.blueletterbible.org/esv/mar/10/1/s_967001.

While the world says, "You are too young to be a parent, you have your whole life ahead of you… It is just a mass of cells you are eliminating from your body. It is your body, do what you want with it. No one has the right to tell you otherwise," Scripture says,

> Blessed be the God and Father of our Lord Jesus Christ, who has blessed us with every spiritual blessing in the heavenly places in Christ, just as He chose us in Him before the foundation of the world, that we would be holy and blameless before Him. In love He predestined us to adoption as sons through Jesus Christ to Himself, according to the kind intention of His will, to the praise of the glory of His grace, which He freely bestowed on us in the Beloved.[18]

> EPHESIANS 1:3–11 (NASB)

"Behold, children are a gift of the LORD, The fruit of the womb is a reward" (Psalm 127:3, NASB).[19]

---

18   "Ephesians 1 (NASB95)," Blue Letter Bible, accessed November 17, 2023, https://www.blueletterbible.org/nasb95/eph/1/1/s_1098001.
19   "Psalm 127 (NASB95)," Blue Letter Bible, accessed November 17, 2023, https://www.blueletterbible.org/nasb95/psa/127/3/s_605003.

"For You formed my inward parts; You wove me in my mother's womb" (Psalm 139:13, NASB).[20]

"Before I formed you in the womb I knew you, And before you were born I consecrated you; I have appointed you a prophet to the nations" (Jeremiah 1:5, NASB).[21]

While the world says, "Physical beauty defines your worth, and you should do all you can to look like a runway model or movie star," Scripture says,

> Your adornment must not be merely external—braiding the hair, and wearing gold jewelry, or putting on dresses; but let it be the hidden person of the heart, with the imperishable quality of a gentle and quiet spirit, which is precious in the sight of God.
>
> 1 PETER 3:3–4 (NASB)

"Charm is deceitful and beauty is vain, But a woman who fears the LORD, she shall be praised" (Proverbs 31:30, NASB).

20   "Psalm 139 (NASB95)," Blue Letter Bible, accessed November 17, 2023, https://www.blueletterbible.org/nasb95/psa/139/3/s_617003.
21   "Jeremiah 1 (NASB95)," Blue Letter Bible, accessed November 17, 2023, https://www.blueletterbible.org/nasb95/jer/1/1/s_746001.

When Samuel was sent by the Lord to find Saul's successor from Jesse the Bethlehemite's family, he looked at all of Jesse's sons and thought that Eliab was the one. He was not the one, and the Lord said to Samuel, "Do not look at his appearance or at the height of his stature, because I have rejected him; for God sees not as man sees, for man looks at the outward appearance, but the LORD looks at the heart" (1 Samuel 16:7, NASB).

David was ruddy, smaller in stature than his other brothers, but considered handsome. He was handpicked and anointed to be king because he was a man after God's heart and a true worshipper who feared the Lord.

The world not only presents the lie that physical beauty is important, but it also tells the lie that your life must always appear perfect and not flawed.

Even as a family grows in their relationship with God, they will fall into this lie.

For example, on Sunday morning, while getting ready for church, the household is rushing, parents are bickering or barely talking, and children are feeling the tension. The car pulls into the church parking lot, everyone gets out of the car and is greeted by others, and all of a sudden, smiles appear, and the appearance turns to one big happy family as they enter the church… Has anyone out there ever experienced this? I have…

Even in our workplace, we might put on a persona that is very put together and sure of our abilities when we really are not that sure of ourselves at all. We tell ourselves that we cannot show weakness or be transparent with our coworkers because we do not want them to have an advantage over us. When we acknowledge our weaknesses and dependence on God, His strength, grace, and favor take over.

> And He has said to me, "My grace is sufficient for you, for power is perfected in weakness." Most gladly, therefore, I will rather boast about my weaknesses, so that the power of Christ may dwell in me. Therefore I am well content with weaknesses, with insults, with distresses, with persecutions, with difficulties, for Christ's sake; for when I am weak, then I am strong.
>
> 2 CORINTHIANS 12:9–10 (NASB)

PRAYER AND OUR POSTURE

"But by the grace of God I am what I am, and His grace toward me did not prove vain; but I labored even more than all of them, yet not I, but the grace of God with me" (1 Corinthians 15:10, NASB).

> Whoever speaks, is to do so as one who is speaking the utterances of God; whoever serves is to do so as one who is serving by the strength which God supplies; so that in all things God may be glorified through Jesus Christ, to whom belongs the glory and dominion forever and ever. Amen.
>
> 1 PETER 4:11 (NASB)

Remember my example of a tsunami, little cracks that spread into destruction. Now, the words below may seem like strong, harsh words, but if you are a Christian and believe or justify your life with the following statement, hear my heart and prayer for you. You are vulnerable to deception that may cause destruction.

I go to church on Sunday and read the Bible, but during the work week, I just do not have time. I give God Sunday...

I can tell you unequivocally that daily consistent time in God's Word must be a priority in your life. He is the giver of time, and He will make way for all things that are necessary for you to accomplish in a day. He will reprioritize your "to-do" list and miraculously give you all the time you need when you put Him first every day. You will be amazed how He honors us when we honor Him first. His Word is the nourishment you need to deal with the current day's troubles and trials. His encouragement will give wisdom, counsel, and instructions to maneuver through the day. Jesus, the Son of God, directs us in Matthew 4:4 when speaking directly to satan that we need to live on every word that comes out of the mouth of God. Once a week is not enough! I am not saying that you need to go to the extreme and ignore life, family, and children in the name of God, but have balance. If you miss a day, God's love and grace are always present. In all circumstances, if Jesus is not the vertical in your life, your horizontal will be much more difficult and filled with deception than it needs to be. Make Jesus the center of all things and seek Him first.

> This book of the law shall not depart from your mouth, but you shall meditate on it day and night,

so that you may be careful to do according to all that is written in it; for then you will make your way prosperous, and then you will have success. Have I not commanded you? Be strong and courageous! Do not tremble or be dismayed, for the LORD your God is with you wherever you go.

JOSHUA 1:8–9 (NASB)

How blessed is the man who does not walk in the counsel of the wicked, Nor stand in the path of sinners, Nor sit in the seat of scoffers! But his delight is in the law of the LORD, And in His law he meditates day and night. He will be like a tree firmly planted by streams of water, Which yields its fruit in its season And its leaf does not wither; And in whatever he does, he prospers.

PSALM 1:1–3 (NASB)

"But He [Jesus] answered and said, 'It is written, "MAN SHALL NOT LIVE ON BREAD ALONE, BUT ON EVERY WORD THAT PROCEEDS OUT OF THE MOUTH OF GOD"'" (Matthew 4:4, NASB).

In conclusion, as you read through and begin to understand and navigate your trauma and grief in healthy ways and you put the ten truths mentioned above into practice, your heart, mind, and spirit will be transformed. Once a foreign concept and attitude, it will now become second nature as you align with the Holy Spirit. Theories, thoughts, and ideas that were attached to you will soon become chaff in the wind. Your foundation will be solid with Jesus at the center as your life-saving anchor. The Bible will be your road map, your GPS for life's decisions and path.

You will enter "Praise the Lord Living" for life!

"Let us examine and probe our ways, And let us return to the LORD" (Lamentations 3:40, NASB).

Take one truth until you master it; you will not get to where you need to be overnight, and you will not be able to undo the past thought patterns, hurt, and trauma and grief overnight. Review each truth and take a moral inventory of your honest feelings toward each one.

What are you opposed to in each truth?

What do you agree with in each truth?

Read each truth again, noting the opposition and agreement. Write out the opposition and agreement.

#1 Truth—*A person cannot say they know God and disregard Jesus.*

#2 Truth—*You are the righteous of God in Christ Jesus.*

#3 Truth—*Satan is not equal to God in power or majesty—he is the opposition of God and His purposes, but does not threaten His power.*

#4 Truth—*We are fighting against powers, principalities, and evil, not people.*

#5 Truth—*Prayer always precedes peace and restoration.*

#6 Truth—*Decrease so that He increases.*

#7 Truth—*Become clay in the hands for the potter.*

#8 Truth—*Light has no fellowship with darkness.*

#9 Truth—*Jesus is the way, the truth, and the life for everyone.*

#10 Truth—*Worldly ways are anti-Christ.*

Refer to a tool I shared earlier, become aware of feelings these truths trigger, pull your mind away from those thoughts that make you feel uncomfortable, be objective, and decide to think about the truths in a new light.

Awareness is the ability to identify the triggers.

Away-ness is the ability to detach from them.

Affirming is deciding to rethink the way you previously thought, renewing your mind.

As you apply awareness, away-ness, and affirm each truth, God will guide your mind and heart to receive His viewpoint, clarity, and understanding. This may increase your shame, but ultimately, it will bring hidden areas into God's light so that He can shatter all the misconceptions you have and experience His grace more fully. Our shame for His grace.

"Search me, O God, and know my heart. Try me and know my anxious thoughts; And see if there be any hurtful way in me, And lead me in the everlasting way" (Psalm 139:23–24, NASB).

🌿 *We Have a Helper—We Are Not Alone!* 🌿

The Holy Spirit gives us the power and encouragement: "I will ask the Father, and He will give you another Helper, that He may be with you forever…I will not leave you as orphans; I will come to you" (John 14:16, 18, NASB).

Once we accept Christ into our hearts and surrender our lives, He sends the Holy Spirit. The Holy Spirit's involvement in our lives as a helper does the following as we begin our relationship with Christ:

1. Pointing out our need for confession

2. Revealing the truth

3. Teaching what we need to know

4. Reminding us of the teachings and examples of Jesus

5. Reminding us of our identity and other gifts in Christ

6. Convicting us of our need for Christ and of specific sins

The Holy Spirit breaks through our denial and shows us what we need to confess and change. Conviction and confession are personal, and it is between you and the Holy Spirit.

Again, King David committed adultery, lied, betrayed a friend who trusted him, and resorted to cold-blooded murder; however, Nathan the prophet confronted David to convict him of his crimes. David was convicted in his heart and repented. In Old Testament times, God used prophets, but after Christ, He uses the Holy Spirit.

❧ *Benefits of Confession* ❧

1. Confession made David a more compassionate person and king.

2. He received great relief and joy from experiencing forgiveness.

3. He gained a deeper love relationship with God.

"All discipline for the moment seems not to be joyful, but sorrowful; yet to those who have been trained by it, afterwards it yields the peaceful fruit of righteousness" (Hebrews 12:11, NASB).

"If we confess our sins, He is faithful and righteous to forgive us our sins and to cleanse us from all unrighteousness" (1 John 1:9, NASB).

Again, the purpose of confession is not payment for our sins; it is the means God has given us so that we can experience forgiveness He has already extended to His children. Jesus' death on the cross paying for our sins completely. Confession brings peace and joy!

If you are at the point where you are confessing sins to God for the first time, you might want to use the following prayer as an example:

> Dear Father,
>
> The Holy Spirit has shown me that I sinned in this way or area... (name sins of thoughts and actions as specific as possible).
>
> I thank You that I am completely forgiven and that You choose not to remember my sins; they are as far as the east is to the west. I realize that You have declared me to be deeply loved, completely forgiven, redeemed, fully pleasing and beautiful in your sight, totally accepted, and a new creature due to the death and resurrection of King Jesus Christ. I am Your child and heir to Your kingdom. I am now a new creature, complete in Jesus and being transformed each day to His image. Amen!

As we come before God to confess our sins, we can do this knowing that our Savior and Lord Jesus Christ was tempted in all areas of life just as we are. Read Hebrews 2:17–18; 4:15–16.

Finally, I want to end this book with the subject of love! I know there are different types of love, different levels, different permissions, and submissions of love that we allow ourselves to give others. God's definition of love is our starting and ending point, our solid foundation for love to grow, nurture, and spread to family, friends, coworkers, and all humankind.

> Love is patient, love is kind and is not jealous; love does not brag and is not arrogant, does not act unbecomingly; it does not seek its own, is not provoked, does not take into account a wrong suffered, does not rejoice in unrighteousness, but rejoices with the truth; bears all things, believes all things, hopes all things, endures all things.
>
> 1 CORINTHIANS 13:4–7 (NASB)

Think of the people you love; do you love them as this scripture above describes? Always, most times, or sometimes? Have you ever experienced this kind of love?

If the above is the foundation and example, and we have never given or received this level of love, then let's start today to change that. To be a person that loves unconditionally and will place another person's well-being above themselves. To love as Jesus loved humanity yesterday, today, and all the days to come.

"Hatred stirs up strife, But love covers all transgressions" (Proverbs 10:12, NASB).

"Above all, keep fervent in your love for one another, because love covers a multitude of sins" (1 Peter 4:8, NASB).

Keeping these two scriptures in mind and our definition of love, we can move forward relating to people in every walk of life, knowing that if we always show love, our faults, failures, mistakes, misgivings, misunderstandings, and misconceptions can be covered by the love we give. Does this mean to intentionally hurt and then show love? *No*!

It means being in a constant state of patience and kindness, not provoking your spouse, children, friends, or coworkers, and not being happy when others fail. Do not be glad of another's misfortunes; be an encouragement and show empathy. Do not keep a record of wrongs in your head and play them over and over when you interact with a person. Take a moment in every situation to pause and respond in love, all that encompasses the word and act of love. Love is a verb, always in action, always evolving and growing, just like us.

We are on a love journey with our Lord and Savior, Jesus, who leads us to the throne room of mercy, where God the Father dwells. He is the epitome of love and grace that we strive to emulate. On that journey, we are given the gift of another person who is traveling alongside us. Our paths with them can be for a day, a week, a year, a decade, or a lifetime. This was predetermined by God before the foundations of the earth for His will and purpose.

What we know for certainty is that God is love, so our journey should leave a footprint and legacy of how we loved ourselves and others, how we received grace and gave it, and how we received and gave forgiveness. The journey will not be smooth, and we will fall, fail, and stumble along more times than anyone would like to admit. It will have enormous climbs, rough waters, and very dark, deep pits that we will need to crawl out of, but without a doubt, if we walk the journey with the Father, Jesus Christ, and the Holy Spirit at our side, as our guide, as our anchor, we will know the truth and reach our destination!

❧ *The Lighter Side of Life* ❧

Now that we have reached our wonderful journey together, I would like to encourage you to take the time to walk outside and take a few moments with the sunrise if you are in the east, sunset if you are in the west, and if you are in the middle of our country surrounded by open plains, find the sunrise or sunset that is the most peaceful.

Stop for a moment, breathe in, and feel the Lord's presence and the peace it will bring.

"Your word is a lamp to my feet And a light to my path" (Psalm 119:105, NASB).

Printed in the USA
CPSIA information can be obtained
at www.ICGtesting.com
LVHW010542280224
772979LV00009B/198